Youth Violence Prevention

Youth Violence Prevention

A Guide for Concerned Parents and Professionals

Lindley E. Bassarath MD

Writers Club Press
San Jose New York Lincoln Shanghai

Youth Violence Prevention
A Guide for Concerned Parents and Professionals

Writers Club Press
an imprint of iUniverse, Inc.

For information address:
iUniverse, Inc.
5220 S. 16th St., Suite 200
Lincoln, NE 68512
www.iuniverse.com

ISBN: 0-595-20819-3

Printed in the United States of America

To Austin,
may you grow up in a safer world.

CONTENTS

ACKNOWLEDGEMENTS

I would like to gratefully acknowledge all the researchers and clinicians who dedicate their lives to understanding, treating and preventing antisocial behaviour in children, adolescents, and adults. Your numerous contributions are all essential in enhancing the quality of these families' lives and our ability to help them.

INTRODUCTION

"Feuding schoolgirl shoots classmate". Unfortunately, headlines like this are no longer unheard of or even rare. This same newspaper article, from March 2001, also documented eight students making bomb threats, a ninth grader shooting two fellow students and injuring 13, two 17 year olds arrested on conspiracy to commit murder, an 18 year old emailing a threat to a school official, a 14 year old threatening to kill three girls, and another 14 year old accused of holding a class hostage.

Violent crime seems to stand out more now, particularly as overall crime rates have fallen and a higher proportion of reported crime is aggressive in nature. Much has been written about crime, punishment, treatment, and now, prevention. The latter will occupy the pages of this book. Youth, parents, schools, the courts, politicians, criminologists, clinicians, researchers, and sociologists, are placing more and more emphasis on violence prevention and health promotion.

Primary prevention, before antisocial behaviour even begins, appears to be most promising in terms of reducing future antisocial behaviour, increasing quality of life for the child and family, as well as reducing victims' and society's ultimate risk and suffering. Right now prevention strategies are largely in the hands of governments, agencies, and academics. But others also can be empowered through knowledge to play an active role in reducing the risk of aggression in children.

Society tends to look for simple formulas to explain complex human behaviors such as violence, antisocial behaviour, or criminality. However, a thorough understanding of the breadth of influences, both within and external to individuals, will enable more thoughtful and comprehensive planning, discussion, and hopefully, action.

Society also tends to look for people or systems to blame for aggression—usually parents, schools, justice system, government, but not always in that order. We tend to look for linear cause and effect relationships between some variable, such as parenting, and some outcome, such as a child shooting another. However, the scientific literature would suggest that there is seldom such a straightforward correlation. We are complex human beings with many influences. This book will hopefully illustrate the many factors impinging on us, in order to give concerned adults the big picture. Only then can effective planning, prevention and intervention take place.

The purpose of this book is to discuss what is known about risk and protective factors for violent and antisocial behavior. Five sets of factors are covered: individual, parental, family, community, and society. The groupings, while convenient, have a great deal of overlap and do intermix to increase or decrease the risk of violence in any one individual. Principal findings from research are stated, implications given, limitations described, and references for further reading provided. Risk factors that increase the risk of violence in a given child are described for each category. These are followed by factors that protect against the development of aggressive behavior. References are listed in brackets.

The way to understand this is to see the multitude of factors that interact to increase or decrease the risk of antisocial behaviour in any child. Violence prevention is a group effort. We can succeed if we critically and objectively look at the contributions of ourselves, our families, neighbourhoods, and society. This isn't easy, but it is necessary to provide an honorable legacy to current and future generations.

CHAPTER ONE: FACTORS RELATED TO THE CHILD

Behavioral Risk Factors
Psychological Risk Factors
School-related Risk Factors
Medical/psychiatric Rick Factors
Other Risk Factors
Protective Factors

A1. Early onset of aggressive behaviour

Onset of physical aggression in children (especially long before the age of 10) has consistently been shown in research to be predictive of later violence in that child (1,2). For these purposes, aggression is defined as any outward destructive behavior; violence refers to outward and intentional use of or threat of use of physical force. Many believe that each individual reaches his or her own characteristic and personal style of aggressive interaction with others from a very young age; further, this individual level of aggressive tendency remains quite stable over time. Much of the research implicates some stability in aggressive behavior from age 6 onwards (3). In one study, first-graders rated as aggressive in the classroom and school were much more likely to have been arrested for violent crime by age 33! Hence early onset can be very predictive of the future.

Implications:

1. This is one of the strongest findings to date; it has been replicated many times. Thus early onset will strongly interact with other individual and family risk factors (see below) to increase the chance of further violence as the child grows.

1

2. Some aggressive behaviour in toddlers can be developmentally normal and expected. However persistence even into preschool may be cause for concern.

3. Many if not most children who were aggressive when younger don't necessarily become violent youth. Thus even early onset of aggression is a changeable risk factor if handled sensitively but firmly by adults.

Limitations:

1. This finding is fairly robust in boys, but less so in girls. This may be due to different socialization and parenting of girls or their generally faster development and acquisition of skills.

2. Early aggression by itself doesn't explain later violence, as they both reflect the same underlying predisposition to aggressive means of handling situations.

3. Many believe that studies have been measuring stability of differences between children rather than stability within any given child (4). Thus life events, social contexts, and other situational variables can substantially modify the life course of a child who has early aggressive tendencies.

A2. Impulse control

A long-term study of 411 boys in working class neighborhoods of Cambridge, England found that impulsivity in childhood was somewhat predictive of later violence when the boys became youth or adults (5). This was true whether the subjects reported the violence themselves or official records were used. Impulsivity is basically defined as "acting without thinking" and many of us do this from time to time. However, some children do this more than others, and some do it as a fairly consistent pattern of behavior. They usually have genuine difficulty controlling their own behavior. Difficulty inhibiting impulses has been linked to poor or immature functioning in the brain's frontal lobe, along with other so-called "executive functions". Children with impulse problems tend to be more emotionally reactive and hostile (6) when they perceive a threat (known as reactive aggression). Other children more carefully plan or choose the targets of their aggression, as in bullying (instrumental aggression).

Implications:

1. Impulsivity may be part of a larger or more pervasive problem, such as Attention Deficit/Hyperactivity Disorder. It is worth ruling this out, since the treatment would differ if ADHD were present.

2. Children can be taught, through cognitive-behavioral therapy or social skills training, to think and reason before acting or at least to inhibit their aggressive or unacceptable impulses.

3. Again, not every impulsive child becomes an aggressive youth. However, in order to function well socially, on the job, and academically, children do need to learn to monitor and control their thoughts and impulses to maintain self-control and earn respect from others.

Limitations:

1. The role of impulsivity by itself only slightly increases a child's risk of future antisocial behaviour. Thus, many other variables will need to be present to add to a child's propensity for ongoing aggression.

2. Impulsivity is actually a difficult thing to measure. While it can be done, usually a laboratory test is not used in longitudinal studies to quantify impulsivity. Thus deciding whether a child is impulsive or not may rely on judgment.

3. It is not always clear from the literature, how many children who are described as "impulsive" have Attention Deficit Hyperactivity

Disorder or other neuropsychiatric conditions that would predispose them to acting prematurely before rational thought kicks in.

A3. Early antisocial behavior

Antisocial behavior is described as violation of the rights of others and social norms. There is now substantial evidence that early antisocial acts by a child are very good predictors of future delinquency (much like early onset of aggression). Examples include stealing by preschool, discipline problems by age 8, and early teenage sexual intercourse or drug selling have all been linked to antisocial and violent behaviors later in life. In one classic study, men with histories of antisocial behavior from ages 6 through 17 were more often charged with robbery, murder and rape as adults than those without such as history. Children who start their antisocial careers early tend to have greater breadth, frequency and severity of antisocial behaviors than children who start later on (e.g. adolescence). For the smaller group that starts young, alcohol abuse, promiscuity, dangerous driving, theft, poor work history and multiple unstable relationships can often be the adolescent and adult patterns of behavior that will emerge (2).

Implications:

1. This is one area where overt behaviour can be picked up early. Prevention of future offending and violence would be greatly enhanced if there are early signs that are recognized and given the significance they deserve.

2. Children at risk tend to expand their repertoire of undesirable behaviors as they grow older. Thus, use of standard parenting techniques such as time out, consequences, or rewards would be prudent but likely insufficient by themselves as children get older.

3. The old adage that "boys will be boys" may be true for some kids (i.e. preschool or elementary), but highly antisocial boys tend to grow up to become antisocial men. This is particularly true if the boys begin to show a general pattern of rule violation and defiance rather than just isolated examples.

Limitations:

1. This finding of early onset of antisocial behaviors does not predict females' antisocial futures as well as males. Girls tend to show their aggression in social ways at first—ostracizing peers, shunning, rumors etc. (7).

2. A child's tendency to demonstrate antisocial behaviors likely interacts with other factors such as peer pressure, impulsivity, role modeling by adults, and parenting style to name a few.

3. Youth who start antisocial behaviors in adolescence are not necessarily risk-free. Up to one quarter of them will continue their delinquent ways beyond the teenage years. The antisocial company that such youth tend to keep helps determine how involved they become in antisocial acts.

A4. Drug use

Early alcohol or drug use, especially before the age of 12, has been linked to greater risk of future antisocial behaviour, in addition to the medical risks posed (8). This tends to apply to most substances currently in recreational use, but particularly to amphetamines, cocaine, PCP (phencyclidine), LSD (Lysergic acid diethylamide), barbiturates, and tranquilizers (9). In addition, some research suggests that even chronic marijuana or opiate use (e.g. heroin) increases the risk of violent behavior. The risk of violence can be influenced by intoxication, withdrawal, crime done to acquire drugs, or involvement in the drug trade (settling debts, dealing with informants, resolving disputes). The proportion of youth with antisocial behavior that also use substances, including alcohol, varies between studies but has been found to be as high as 91%! (10) Some studies indicate that antisocial behavior precedes drug use. However, the opposite can also be true.

Implications:

1. Early substance use and abuse has multiple pathways to future violence or criminality. Drugs cost money; they can involve dealers, other users, and can go hand in hand with criminality.

2. Early treatment and prevention can help decrease risk of future dependency as well as delinquency. Again, preventing a downward spiral, much like intervening in early onset of aggression, is much better than the medical, social and societal costs down the road.

3. Substance use can either intensify emotions such as anger, or inhibit emotions such as shame or guilt. Either scenario can increase the potential for violence, particularly in those who are impulsive, reactive, intoxicated or withdrawing from substances.

Limitations:

1. Substance use often interacts with or masks other problems such as anxiety or depressive symptoms. The underlying problem, if there is one, should also be attended to and treated.

2. Drugs are only one cause amongst many for crime. Certainly not everyone who uses drugs or alcohol has antisocial tendencies or behaviors.

3. More needs to be understood about the situational variables and contexts under which drugs exert influence and increase potential for antisocial behavior such as violence.

A5. Alcohol use

Alcohol has several potential relationships with crime and violence. First, individuals with impulsive personalities tend to have a high rate of alcohol problems (11); poor impulse control, as discussed later, is associated with violent crime. Second, between 40% and 56% of violent adult offenders have had an alcohol abuse problem. Many of them started quite young, both in terms of alcohol abuse, as well as their criminal careers. Surveys of adolescent offenders indicate low rates of alcohol use at the actual time of their offence (12). Third, the consumption of alcohol has also been found to increase the violence risk in situations of potential conflict. Finally, there is some evidence that some families with alcohol abuse and aggressive behavior may have a genetic predisposition to both, especially the males (13). Thus with all of this evidence, adolescent use of alcohol, especially if frequent and/or excessive, is worrisome for many reasons.

Implications:

1. Families with a history of alcohol abuse should watch for signs in the younger generation. Children and youth, who have parents with alcohol problems, have at least 3 times the risk of having such a problem themselves.

2. Alcohol or other drug use may be masking an underlying problem, such as anxiety, depression, Post Traumatic Stress Disorder, or Attention Deficit/Hyperactivity Disorder among others.

3. Due to the high association in adulthood between alcohol and crime, much prevention of later damage can potentially be done if one is vigilant to this risk factor in youth.

Limitations:

1. The robust findings in adults have not really panned out in children and adolescents. While alcohol use is certainly concerning in the

young, the degree to which it independently contributes to violence in adolescence is controversial.

2. Much of the above research is based on self-report by the subject. This means, for example, that adolescents, as well as adults could actually be underreporting their alcohol consumption.

3. It is not clear how much of alcohol use in youth at risk is based on genetics from their families of origin, modeling, social context (e.g. peers) or other influences.

A6. Early cigarette use

Although nicotine is technically a drug or "substance", cigarettes deserve special mention. This is because early onset of smoking cigarettes (before age 14 in one study) has been linked with later onset of violent behavior in youth (5). This is particularly true when combined with a constellation of antisocial behaviors and use of other substances. Once they reach adulthood, people with impulsive personalities tend to have up to triple the rate of smoking when compared to others without impulsiveness in their personality makeup. Youth who smoke cigarettes light up for many reasons—for stimulation, relaxation, to bond with a peer group, impress others, relieve boredom etc. However, it is fairly clear from research that the early use of substances such as cigarettes, alcohol, and other drugs can be associated with disruptive and antisocial behaviors in young people, especially when combined with other risk factors.

Implications:

1. Young people continue to need much education about the harmful effects of cigarette smoking. These include not only health effects, but social and behavioral ones as well.

2. As parents, one incentive to reduce one's cigarette intake is hopefully the suggestion that children who pick up the habit when young may be at higher risk for other associated difficulties, including aggression and criminality.

3. Many people tend to not stop at cigarettes. Thus, cigarette smoking may be accompanied by other drug or alcohol use. Thus parents need to be vigilant for such behaviors as they can occur at the same time.

Limitations:

1. Not everyone who starts smoking when young is going to develop violent behavior or a criminal career. The risk noted is an increased risk as a group compared to others who did not start to smoke early if at all.

2. People can often start when young and quit early as well. Harm reduction (reducing gradually to lowest possible level of use) can also minimize the damage. Further, it is not at all clear how much one has to smoke to increase one's risk of later antisocial behavior.

3. Violent behavior is too complex to be explained by one factor alone. Likely cigarette smoking adds to other risk factors such as peer group, lack of monitoring, school problems or others.

B1. Difficult temperament

10-20% of children are born with a "difficult temperament" (14). This is defined as being highly active, impulsive, short in attention span, fearless, moody, having difficulty with change, and problems with regulation of emotions and habits (such as feeding or sleeping). These characteristics are the innate inborn temperamental traits of these children's personalities. These children are more at risk to show behavioral problems such as lack of cooperativeness, aggression, poor social skills, and diminished academic performance (15). Difficult temperament is sometimes maligned as having more to do with the perception and poor coping style of the parent, usually the mother, in research. However, the parents usually know their child best as they are the ones who live together!

Implications:

1. A child who has a difficult temperament increases the stress level in parents and families. As a result, parents can through stress or exhaustion be inconsistent or physically punitive. Unfortunately, this actually can increase a child's aggressive tendencies.

2. No one is to blame for a child's temperamental disposition. He or she was likely born that way as such things are under a great deal of biological/genetic control. But how that child is dealt with is under adult control.

3. Adults will very likely need extra support, resources, and advice to effectively keep them out of the power struggles with these children and help them succeed. Temperamentally difficult children are very challenging, but can also be very rewarding and fascinating as they develop.

Limitations:

1. There is controversy about how different adults, whether they be parents, strangers or researchers, rate a child's temperament. Thus the real question becomes is temperament really fixed or can it be expressed differently, depending on context, relationship, or attachment to the adult.

2. Temperament fairly quickly interacts with a child's environment and experience of parenting to develop into the child's emerging

personality. Thus it can become difficult over time to tease out what was inborn and what was acquired.

3. Because children often behave differently in different contexts, getting reports from different environments (friends, schools, home, extracurricular activities) can provide a more comprehensive picture of a child's functioning.

B2. Intelligence Quotient (IQ)

Numerous studies using psychological IQ testing have found that antisocial youth and adults have a higher "Performance IQ" than "Verbal IQ". This means that they may have trouble at times with spoken or written language. Both IQs together make up what is typically called IQ. In violent juveniles, the difference between verbal IQ and performance IQ is as much as 17 points! (16). The verbal problems tend to precede antisocial behaviour particularly in the presence of Attention Deficit/Hyperactivity Disorder. The low verbal intelligence may contribute by making it harder to verbally communicate and may enable the child to elicit negative feedback or interactions from peers or family. These children aren't necessarily any less smart or bright than nonviolent children, but they can have specific vulnerability in speech/language comprehension or expression.

Implications:

1. Like other learning problems, early speech or language problems can be identified and helped. Speech therapy or other academic programming can be quite useful in helping these children succeed.

2. The consistency in research of this verbal deficit finding, makes it quite important to help the child with verbal problems; this by itself may lessen the child's frustration and subsequent aggressive behaviour.

3. Families who have a member or members with a history of learning problems are at higher risk of having children with speech or academic problems.

Limitations:

1. As it is not clear the link between verbal problems and antisocial behavior, one should not assume that one causes the other. In any event, language difficulties deserve recognition in their own right.
2. Early identification and therapy or academic programming for any speech/language problem may not by itself be enough to alter a child's course of antisocial behaviour, depending on the presence of other risk factors.
3. IQ testing is controversial. This is particularly true when one considers whether multicultural influences are accurately accounted for and interpreted by standardized testing.

B3. Cultural sensitivity/diversity issues

Today's communities are much less homogeneous than they used to be. Globalization, instant communication, and the movement of people have added richness ("diversity") to our societal matrix. One of the areas in which this plays a role is in gang activity. Some gangs organize around specific sociocultural groups, although many have looser associations. Sometimes gang warfare and related "turf" issues explode between culturally different groups. Further, many societal groups (women, visible minorities, and homosexuals to name a few) have experienced violent hate crimes. Some innovative attempts at changing such closed-mindedness are occurring. Initiatives that educate students about prejudice, working with different cultures and values, and encourage openness are becoming more common in schools and communities (17). In some programs, police offi-cers are involved in the teaching, which encourages more collaboration between citizens and law enforcement. Such issues can also be discussed and promoted in the home.

Implications:

1. Prejudice and the intolerance of others' religious and cultural beliefs is increasingly being targeted for intervention in the community and schools.

2. Promotion of healthy, prosocial values that embrace difference, as opposed to resisting it, can be practiced in any setting—home, school, office, community.

3. Intolerance and discrimination are learned behaviors. They can be unlearned as well, decreasing the risk of marginalization of youth towards gangs of like-minded culturally rigid individuals.

Limitations:

1. Not all gangs are necessarily based on sociocultural ideologies. Gangs exist for many reasons, some of them largely economic.

2. It is not clear yet from the research how successful we are being over the long-term in actually preventing youth from joining gangs in the first place.

3. It is not clear from the literature what the overall impact of multicul-tural intolerance is on the genesis of crime in our society. It is often difficult to tease out from statistics whether crimes are hate-related and/or based on some other motivation.

B4. Risk taking

Many children are "daredevils" in their approach to life. Often children are dared by other children and do risky and dangerous things, such as fighting, "extreme" sports, or theft. Such risk-taking behavior in childhood has been linked to later violent behavior in adolescence (18). It is thought by some that children prone to daring behavior need stimulation because they are often physiologically underaroused and intellectually bored. Some of them have been found to have much lower heart rates than children who do not exhibit such risky behavior (19). This is related to the concept of "fearlessness" mentioned later in the section on anxiety, especially given it is unlikely that anxious children would be daring in their approach to dangerous situations or challenges. In addition, children who take physical risks are at greater risk of injury, particularly head injury, which further increases their risk of impulsive problems.

Implications:

1. Children who are prone to daring or risky behaviors require much stimulation and supervision. They can get up to dangerous activities and consequences unless their sensation-seeking natures are nurtured in more prosocial ways (e.g. athletics, leadership roles etc.)

2. Children who exhibit risky behaviors may also be prone to such things as attention or hyperactive difficulties (ADHD) and this should be looked for and identified if present.

3. Impulsiveness and risk taking may go hand in hand. The consequences of daring behavior are often not fully appreciated or thought through. Cognitive behavioral therapy has been shown to be helpful in giving children problem-solving skills to think about consequences and check their aggressive impulses.

Limitations:

1. Risk taking may need to be present with other risk factors, such as peer influence, opportunity, or ADHD to be fully expressed.

2. What is happening biologically to a child prone to risk taking has not been entirely worked out. Some may have lower heart rates (arousal levels) but this so far appears to be less prominent in those from high risk families and backgrounds.

3. Risk taking can be a healthy part of life. Many very successful people often take "calculated" risks in order to get ahead in life, business or relationships. Life would be somewhat boring if there weren't people with initiative around.

B5. Antisocial beliefs

An individual's attitudes have been found to predict later aggressive behavior. In particular, attitudes favoring use of violence, hostility towards police, and dishonesty have been linked to violent behavior in males. It is thought that such beliefs come about quite early, similar to early onset of aggression (20). Early childhood defiance of rules and lying, especially if persistent could be precursors to later antisocial beliefs and behavior (21). Such belief systems, similar to those of cultural intolerance mentioned previously, can be unfortunately quite stable over time due to the young age at which they were instilled or condoned. Nevertheless, many programs are now attempting to intervene at the level of thinking of children and adolescents—changing attitudes favorable to rule breaking, violence, cheating, and conflict with authority. Certainly as children mature, they need more positive values to succeed socially and on the job.

Implications:

1. Universal values such as honesty, compliance with authority, and non-violence can be easily and successfully distilled in the home and elsewhere. The opportunities for practice abound more in home life as the child grows, before he/she separates in adolescence to practice with peers.

2. Many schools are bringing in universal value-based curricula. These have been shown to be successful in preventing later violence, especially when begun early.

3. Parents can do a fair degree of modeling here, especially in their own dealings with authority or other friends, family, colleagues, and professionals. Children will learn by observation.

Limitations:

1. Much of what is considered a "universal value" is determined by society. Thus being counter to authority has been some source of pride since the post- World War II era (especially during the 1960s).

2. Children do need to learn to think for themselves. Not every rule is necessarily a good rule. They hopefully are encouraged to evaluate rules in context and discuss them openly.

3. The discussion of "universal values" is different and distinct from other value systems (e.g. "Family Values"). This is because universal values such as truth, honesty, or non-violent conflict resolution should not be tied to any particular ideology, but shared by all.

B6. Lack of empathy

Empathy is defined as acknowledgement of feelings and impact of one's behavior on others. A disturbing trend from American crime statistics is that homicides are becoming more and more emotionally detached. Youth who commit murder are using more guns, which enable killing from a distance (22). No physical, emotional or eye contact is necessary. The percentage of youth that kill family members is declining while the proportion that kill complete strangers is increasing. This could imply more emotional disconnection from victims. One proposed developmental pathway suggests that children who have poor or difficult temperament with low empathy at age 2, can show cruelty to animals as well as rule and minor legal violations by age 8, minor delinquency such as shoplifting by age 12, violence by age 20, and spousal abuse, child abuse, and alcoholism in adulthood (23). Thus poor empathy as a child becomes one important feature in a sequentially long career of antisocial behavior.

Implications:

1. Teaching children empathy can be an important ingredient of emerging social skills.

2. Early signs of poor empathy, especially callous and unemotional traits, may predict later trouble and poorer response to treatment (24).

3. As mentioned with antisocial beliefs and social skills, poor empathy may be linked with a belief system involving self-centeredness as opposed to emotional connection to others. Having increasing rates of stranger victims may be another correlate of our society's emphasis on the individual, rather than the collective needs of others.

Limitations:

1. Poor empathy by itself doesn't necessarily lead to a life of crime. It is not known if poor empathy is a cause in and of itself or a result of the interaction of childhood temperament with other experiences.

2. It is not clear how empathy operates in aggression with females. One could argue that aggressive females' tendency to shun and ostracize other girls is a product of emotional disconnection and poor empathy.

3. It is not clear if one's level of empathy is actually changeable. Social skills training usually includes empathy training. However, such interventions have not been shown by themselves to enable all children and youth to be more prosocial and less antisocial. Thus more comprehensive approaches are needed.

B7. Low Reward Dependence

Reward dependence refers to the degree of need (dependence) for social reward or acknowledgement. Thus, a personality characterized by being aloof and extremely independent in thinking and actions may be characterized as having low reward dependence. Having "low" reward dependence, especially when linked with other personality variables such as impulsiveness, quick temper, fearlessness, and risk taking (see above) would collectively comprise what would be typically described as an antisocial personality (25). Being aloof and independent may distinguish one's character as having different goals and values in general from those who are more sociable. Capacities for shame, guilt, and empathy also thought to be lower with such personality traits. While some degree of independence is not a bad thing, some people can be extreme in socially inappropriate or clinically dysfunctional ways.

Implications:

1. Encouraging socialization can lead to great social skills, friendships, and facilitation of one's goals. Most things in life require help or

cooperation from others. The quote "no man is an island" does have some merit.

2. Children who are rejected by peers and become socially isolated for whatever reason may be more prone to violence. Early detection and intervention would be warranted in this event. Some of the youth involved in recent school shootings would fit this profile.

3. Youth who are aloof may be suffering from other psychological or psychiatric problems such as social anxiety, paranoia, early psychosis, depression or others. Clinical assessment may then be indicated.

Limitations:

1. Aloofness and independence can be strengths as well. The ability to "think outside the box" or go against the flow can be useful when people have a herd mentality or exhibit rigid thinking.

2. Reward dependence needs other personality dimensions noted to achieve worrisome significance in terms of violence risk. The others are mentioned above. They are technically known as "Harm Avoidance" (fearlessness) and "Novelty Seeking" (quick temper, impulsiveness).

3. The 3 traits described (reward dependence, harm avoidance, novelty seeking) are thought to be temperamental traits, implying they are stable throughout life. They may have a biological or genetic basis and thus it is not clear if intervention can actually change these individual characteristics.

B8. High self esteem

It is widely believed that low self-esteem is a predisposing factor to aggressive and antisocial behavior. Low self-esteem can indeed result from a child's chronic exposure to high levels of violence (26). However, in terms of the risk of aggressive behavior, some studies have actually found that self-esteem itself is irrelevant to aggression. Further, research suggests that the threat to unduly high self-esteem (also known as narcissism) actually increases the risk of violence towards the source of the insult (27), especially if self-esteem is unstable (can fluctuate depending on outside influence). This means that people who have high but unstable narcissism view themselves supremely; they don't handle challenges and criticisms well and could then become aggressive due to the perception of threat (28). By the way, it is not clear whether teaching or increasing self-esteem necessarily leads to narcissism, but it could in theory.

Implications:

1. Looking for low self-esteem in kids and youth who have antisocial or aggressive behaviors may be the opposite of what one should look for. Narcissism in youth may be a more appropriate target for assessment and intervention.

2. Children should have healthy and realistic not over-inflated and egotistical view of themselves. Sometimes a little humility can be quite therapeutic. In fact, others usually don't like youth or adults who are narcissistic.

3. Children are generally quite self-centered at a very young age. It thus becomes difficult but important as an adult to give the child realistic but sensitive feedback about their real strengths, capabilities and wishes.

Limitations:

1. Research into the roles of self-concept and self-esteem is very recent. Findings should be considered preliminary until more replicated and established.

2. Much research has been done in adults and whether this can be extrapolated towards the child population is highly debatable. However, self-esteem, like other aspects of character, develops over time and the precursors are there in childhood.

3. The causes and evolution of narcissism and over-inflated self-esteem have not been fully articulated from a research point of view. There could be many pathways, some of which may be related to one's temperament and thus hard to change.

B9. Attachment

Insecure attachment in children has been found to be a risk factor, particularly in families already stressed and at high-risk (29). In insecurely attached relationships, the relationship between infants and their caregivers may be characterized by many different features. In the child/parent interaction, these may include anxiety, insensitivity, rejection, avoidance, lack of emotional bond, difficulties with separating from the parent, and difficulties with new people or situations (for example, fussy or aggressive behaviors upon change in routine). In particular families with more stress can have their parenting and attachments to their children affected into toddler-hood and beyond. This has not been found as much in families who don't struggle with poverty and have access to greater resources. Also, this finding linking attachment with aggression has been more marked in male infants than in females.

Implications:

1. Predominant attachment style (especially secure versus insecure) gets established as early as infancy. Once set it may stay consistent as the child grows.

2. Children whose families have many social and economic resources are probably protected by those resources even if they have insecure attachments. Thus families without such support need as much social contact, parenting help, and advocacy as they can get to protect their children from developing and maintaining an insecure attachment.

3. Parent management help and training can modify the course of attachment and subsequent behavior. Good parenting programs tend to emphasize not only how to discipline children, but even more importantly how to build a healthy, secure and affectionate relationship with them.

Limitations:

1. The findings about insecure attachment predicting later behavioral problems are much more consistent in boys than girls. It is not yet clear from research why this is so. why this is so.

2. Many of the research findings are based on experimental laboratory-like study designs. Whether these artificial scenarios reflect real-life attachment conditions is debatable.

3. Attachment isn't necessarily a static, non-changing thing. Infants may start out with one pattern (such as secure attachment), and due to family circumstances or stressors become more insecure over time. The opposite may hopefully also be true.

B10. Stubbornness

Stubbornness has been found to be one of the first steps in the so-called "authority conflict" pathway towards antisocial behavior. Stubbornness and its close relative, defiance, can start very young. Most parents have heard the word "no" from their toddler many times! This is fine, as it is developmentally appropriate while the toddler negotiates his or her way around the world. However, even toddlers and certainly older children need to have firm, consistent but loving limits and consequences set. Otherwise, the potential is there for increasing disobedience and defiance progressing to rule violations such as opposition to teachers, truancy, staying out late, running away and later difficulties with police, bosses, and other relationships. Thus persistent stubbornness can be a sign of and prelude to increasingly serious conflict with adults and authority figures (30).

Implications:

1. Early and persistent stubbornness may be a harbinger of things to come with the family, school, and adults in general. If it persists beyond toddlerhood, further advice may be indicated around parenting techniques to curb this unwanted behavior.

2. Even in the toddler years, children need to know who is in control without power struggles. This is a fine art that involves balancing negotiation, choices, respect, and firmness.

3. Giving a toddler control sometimes, over non safety-related issues for example, may increase his or her willingness be agreeable when the adult really needs control (e.g. if the child is doing something dangerous).

Limitations:

1. For some boys, stubbornness can be merely a phase. The oppositional and stubborn behaviors may be short-lived without progressing to serious antisocial problems.

2. It has not been firmly established whether this authority conflict pathway applies equally if at all to females as they grow up.

3. Many violent youth follow several antisocial pathways simultaneously. These can include authority conflict, overt (aggressive) pathway, and

covert (lying and stealing) pathways (31). However, there is debate about the number of possible routes to later criminal behavior.

B11. Social information processing

Social information processing is a fancy term describing how children interpret the social cues of people around them. It has been found that aggressive children read others' social cues less than non-aggressive children (32). Further, when unsure of others, they don't seek extra information as frequently as other children. Very importantly, they often misinterpret body language or verbal statements as being hostile or threatening, even when this isn't the case. Further, aggressive children may value and desire goals such as control, power or domination more than goals dealing with enhancing relationships with others. They also have access to fewer potential responses, other than aggressive ones, to social situations. Finally, they tend to think that the outcomes of their aggressive acts are more positive than they really are in terms of rewards, social approval, and feeling positive about themselves.

Implications:
1. Aggressive children make these so-called "cognitive errors" at many stages when involved in relationships with other children. Cognitive behavioral therapy has been shown to be of assistance in detecting, changing and rewarding more prosocial means of dealing with people and situations (33).
2. Asking or discovering a child's motive for aggressive behavior can be revealing. If pursued, the source of the misperception can be found; for example, the child likely needs more information about why someone looked at him "funny" before concluding that this person was against him.

3. Early detection and intervention is vital because as the aggressive child grows into adolescence, how they respond to the perceived and real threats of the world becomes more fixed and difficult to change.

Limitations:

1. Although children's misperceptions can lead to rejection by peers, not all aggressive children are rejected nor are all children with social problems aggressive.

2. The origins of how children come to process information in their own ways is not well understood. How children develop their thinking patterns needs to be further researched.

3. The research on effects of therapy on children's cognitive and information-processing systems is in its infancy. More needs to be evaluated on the specific effects of therapy on children's perceptions and aggressive behavior.

B12. Attention-seeking behavior

One very interesting research finding has been that persistent attention seeking at the age of 12 months was found to be very highly related to noncompliance from the child by 18 months of age. This noncompliance was then correlated with aggressive behavior by the child at 24 months of age (34). Then in turn, the aggression at two years was followed by behavior problems (such as temper tantrums, defiance, etc.) by 3 years of age. Of course we have seen that early behavioral problems (such as by age 3) is already known to be connected to future and persistent behavior problems in school and teenage years. Thus, while this should be taken in context, children who continuously need, seek out, and demand attention at a very early age (one year) may indeed be at higher risk for future aggression and behavior problems. In addition to being stressful for the parent, persistent demands for attention may be a clue that preventative steps are necessary.

Implications:

1. One year olds who require constant attention likely need some combination of stimulation and reassurance. While one should strive to be emotionally available to children, it is impossible for most people to continuously engage a child 24 hours a day.

2. A parent with such a child who is demanding, often needs extra support from friends, extended family members or community resources (drop-ins/daycare). These may lessen the stress and increase the child's capacity to be with others, which may actually enhance the quality of parent-child relationship.

3. Having siblings or other similarly aged children may help to spread out the attention. However, having several one-year olds in the room likely requires surveillance from more than one caregiver!

Limitations:

1. Not all children who seek attention at an early age necessarily turn out to be overly aggressive youngsters and adolescents.

2. The research given was done by observational methods alone. Life circumstances and experiences also greatly influence a child's course of development.

3. This sequence of behaviors and findings appears to be more valid for boys than girls.

C1. Learning problems

Academic difficulties are cognitive problems different from social information processing. Early learning problems, disabilities or deficits (however one would like to label them) have been associated with increased risk for long-term antisocial behaviour in vulnerable children (35). Specifically, problems in verbal speech, receptive understanding of language, reading, writing, dyslexia, visual-spatial abilities (which relate to difficulties in perceiving social cues and developing social skills) and memory are prevalent in children and adolescents with behavioral problems (9). How these academic problems actually relate to antisocial behaviour is still a matter of much debate. The presence of these difficulties likely just adds another layer of stress and poor functioning to an already vulnerable child. Learning problems tend to be inborn, biologically based deficits that can be helped once identified and addressed in school and at home.

Implications:

1. If possible, evaluation (such as psychoeducational testing), for presence of special learning needs would greatly aid in detection, planning and understanding of the child's abilities, especially in the presence of academic or behavioral problems.

2. Other cognitive problems, such as Attention Deficit/Hyperactivity Disorder frequently occur with learning problems and should be looked for as well.

3. Children with learning problems can often be neglected, teased, bullied, or rejected socially by their peers much more readily than those without special academic needs. This peer rejection may also increase a child's risk for acting out in an aggressive manner.

Limitations:

1. It is not well understood how cognitive difficulties increase the risk for later aggression. One possibility is that a child's ability to express feelings, put words to thoughts and impulses, or internally regulate their own behaviour ("self-talk") may be compromised.

2. In an ideal world, all children with learning and behavioral problems would receive comprehensive assessments. However, these are not frequently available due to limited resources. Hence early identification may increase the possibility of an academic assessment for learning needs before the child falls far behind academically.

3. Language and reading disorders have been associated with some brain findings in neuroimaging studies (e.g. CAT scan, functional Magnetic Resonance Imaging). Actual differences have been found in different brain regions between children with such problems and those without. This should not however, imply fixed and unchangeable deficits for any given child.

C2. School attitudes

It has been found that a poor attachment or commitment to school is associated with a higher risk of later criminality in youth and adults (36). While the research is inconsistent on this subject, having low educational aspirations in adolescence also have been associated with later violence. A strong, enduring, and supported attachment to a school and schooling has been shown to be one of the most important protective factors against anti-social behavior in youth. Of course, strong bonding to a school is dependent on many other things, such as academic potential, parental support, school environment, school resources, social skills, presence of learning problems or ADHD to name just a few of the issues involved. Thus, children who stay bonded to their educational experience will hopefully avoid or minimize the potential for later trouble. Similarly, youth who change schools frequently are also at higher risk for adolescent violence.

Implications:

1. Parents should encourage a positive attitude towards school, teachers, and learning. This is particularly important as the child enters teenage years, when other influences become more prominent.

2. Parents who work with the school will help children to stay involved and committed towards their own education. A strong alliance between parent, teacher, principal, and school can go a long way towards early identification of problems and support for a child in his or her educational setting.

3. Underlying learning problems, mental health problems such as depression or drug use, as well as school environmental problems (gangs, bullying etc.), could be interfering with the child's enjoyment, success, and attachment to his or her school.

Limitations:

1. The finding of poor bonding leading to later violence has been found more in American students than those who attend European schools. Thus the importance of other cultural or societal factors may be under-recognized.

2. Not all studies have linked school bonding with later antisocial offending by youth. Nevertheless, commitment to education and schooling has many other benefits than just avoidance of a criminal career.

3. It is not clear whether the link between poor school commitment and later crime is just a random association by chance, a causal relationship, or represents other factors. For example, it could be measuring things such as educational achievement level, truancy etc.

C3. School performance

Poor academic performance and school failure have consistently predicted later antisocial behavior and delinquency. In one study, poor academic achievement assessed at age 7 and then again by age 14, was correlated to increased violent offending by teenage years in both boys and girls (37). Switching or being allocated to a lower academic school track was similarly found to be associated with increased risk of criminality in youth and adulthood (5). Poor academic performance has not only been linked to the overall rate of delinquency, but also to increasing frequency and seriousness of the offending behavior. School attitudes and performance probably act together and thus need close attention, particularly in the elementary school years before truancy, drop out, and academic failure occur.

Implications:

1. Academic underachievement is detectable by early elementary school. Thus, it really behooves parents and schools to work together to identify, support, and strengthen a child's academic abilities and problem areas.

2. Many children with disruptive behaviors have other reasons for school failure other than lack of motivation and interest. Learning problems may go unacknowledged and unaddressed for years before everyone begins a search for the "cause" of failure.

3. Nurturing the highest level of academic achievement and potential in any child can go a long way towards keeping him or her on the right track academically and behaviorally.

Limitations:

1. Many children don't do particularly well in school, but don't necessarily get into legal problems either. The two may be associated in studies, but one can't say that academic failure directly causes delinquency.

2. Many children who aren't inclined towards the academic structure of school can nevertheless be very creative in other ways, and achieve much during the course of their lives.

3. Many valued jobs are available that don't necessarily require the highest level of academic education. A love of learning is likely as or more important in today's fast-paced world than the actual marks children get.

C4. Truancy

A high truancy rate in the teenage years has been associated with later or concurrent adolescent violence and offending behaviors (5). Particularly between ages 12 and 14, truancy is problematic not only because of the risk of antisocial behaviour, but also likely because of the company the youth keep when they are truant. Hanging out with other truant youth without any monitoring may be a recipe for trouble. Truancy of course may be due to many reasons, not only poor school attitude and lack of commitment. Many youth, perhaps due to learning disabilities or Attention Deficit/Hyperactivity Disorder simply cannot stay focussed or interested enough and thus begin cutting classes in frustration. Besides, they usually find something more subjectively interesting or rewarding to do with their spare time. Keeping children and youth in school should be a high priority for both parents and the education system.

Implications:

1. Truancy is often one of the last signs of academic underachievement or poor school commitment. Thus by then a real search for underlying causes is necessary, in addition to finding out what the youth does with his or her time.

2. Sometimes the structured school settings may not be suitable for children with special academic needs, such as learning problems. If truancy is an issue, then investigation of alternative schools, tutoring, or psychoeducational testing if indicated should be part of the conversation with the school or school board.

3. Youth, particularly in younger teenage years need to be monitored when out of school; otherwise they can easily find trouble. School provides not only an educational function, but enables everyone to know where a student actually is!

Limitations:

1. Truancy may be a marker for other things noted above, such as poor school attitude, academic underachievement, learning problems, or ADHD.

2. Other issues such as depression or social anxiety should also be considered as potential contributors to truancy. Truancy by itself does not necessarily imply antisocial behaviour is the cause or result.

3. The right academic and supportive environment would ideally enable a child to feel comfortable with his or her class and achieve at a rewarding pace. The fact that this is not always available isn't the child's fault.

C5. Early school dropout

Leaving school prior to the age of 15 in one study was predictive of later teenage violence, adult violence, and convictions for violent offenses (5).

This was found by both self-reports of the study subjects as well as official criminal records. Similarly, entry into the work force either prior to the age of 18 or prior to completion of high school education, has been linked to increased delinquent behaviour, greater substance use, and decrease in earning potential; this was relative to those who achieved their high school diploma or delayed entry into the work force until their adult years (38). While the research may vary as to how young an adolescent has to be to be at greater risk of criminality, the message if fairly clear: those who leave early achieve less and incur more convictions and mental health difficulties (e.g. substance use) compared to those who finish their schooling.

Implications:

1. Finishing one's high school education should be a high priority for many reasons - self-esteem, achievement, later work earnings, lower substance use, and fewer criminal convictions.

2. Finding a way to keep children in school, as with the truancy issue, is an excellent way to prevent later problems and promote healthy, responsible behaviour and achievement. This may involve looking at the same learning, educational, and school-setting issues previously discussed.

3. It is much more difficult to finish one's schooling later in life due to other pressures of family and job. Even though youth sometimes don't feel the need to think much about the future, they may come to regret not finishing their schooling while they have the chance and time.

Limitations:

1. These findings, as with much research, are based on group data. Thus we don't know if a given youth who drops out early is necessarily at higher risk for criminal behaviour. Other factors need to be considered.

2. While it is more difficult, many people do finish their education later in life and can achieve success and satisfaction regardless of earlier school termination.

3. Some people very successfully combine school with an early work career. Many successful entrepreneurs worked very hard as teenagers while completing their high school education.

D1. Brain injury

Trauma to the brain is devastating to the individual and family. It can also predispose one to be more violent with others (39). The most common aggressive clinical syndrome involves violent outbursts with minimal, if any, provocation from others. This can show up as rage attacks, irrational thinking, and violence (40). Another pattern involves poor functioning in the frontal lobes of the brain with corresponding difficulties in inhibiting aggressive impulses and poor reasoning abilities. In several studies, over 60% of violent juvenile offenders had a traumatic head injury in their medical history (41). This was often confirmed by physical exam and CAT scan. The neurologic lesion may not necessarily have been traumatic, as other brain abnormalities can also alter personality. Fortunately, these are not common in children.

Implications:

1. Families require extra support and often respite care (relief) when looking after individuals with traumatic neurological injuries.

2. Anyone with the above aggressive symptoms likely needs medical attention, particularly if there has been a history of head injury. Medication can often be of great assistance with such difficulties as explosive temper due to brain trauma.

3. The role of more subtle, repetitive head injury, such as repeated accidents, falls, or child abuse is likely underestimated.

Limitations:

1. Head injury has been related in the literature to violent behaviour, but not general or non-violent antisocial behaviour.

2. The numbers of subjects in studies related to brain injury are generally small and need to be interpreted with caution. Further, many studies have used self-report of subjects without corroboration from physical exam or neurological investigation (such as CT or MRI scan).

3. Neurologically challenged offenders in these studies were not always directly compared to those without brain injury to test for differences.

D2. Attention Deficit/Hyperactivity Disorder (ADHD)

ADHD is present in approximately 3%-5% of children. Almost 50% of adolescents who suffer from ADHD also exhibit antisocial symptoms (42). It is fairly clear from the research that the presence of early childhood aggression and ADHD predicts a much longer and difficult course of antisocial behavior in youth (43). It also makes treatment efforts more problematic with poorer follow-through, resistance to treatment and lack of compliance with treatment. While the best treatment packages for these youth may reduce their overt aggressive symptoms and future legal involvement, they can still have many problems in their families, schooling and relationships. To achieve a diagnosis of ADHD, either inattentive or hyperactive/impulsive symptoms have to be present in more than one setting before the age of 7. Thus ADHD is diagnosable and treatable early before school and behavioral problems become more intractable.

Implications:

1. Early detection and intervention with children suffering from ADHD can help prevent a whole host of other problems, including violent behavior and subsequent legal involvement.

2. The children who have difficulties with inattention, hyperactivity, and impulsivity simultaneously are most at risk and definitely deserve thorough assessment and treatment.

3. Treatment includes medication, parenting advice and support (since the behaviors are difficult to handle), as well as behavioral interventions in the school setting. A team approach including parent, school and mental health professional(s) is best.

Limitations:

1. The combination of ADHD and early antisocial behavior is felt by some researchers to be a prelude to psychopathic and sociopathic behavior. This is debatable and may preclude hopeful intervention and support for families.

2. The best treatments for ADHD have been under considerable study with a huge study (the Multimodal Treatment for ADHD study of nearly 600 children) being analyzed for results. More recommendations will be gradually forthcoming from this work (44).

3. Research data is only recently emerging about the course of antisocial behavior when early antisocial and ADHD symptoms are addressed. We really don't have enough information about what happens with early intervention in this area.

D3. Psychiatric disorder

Mental illness is extremely common in violent youth. ADHD is present in up to one-half of youth with antisocial behavior (42). Mood disorders, particularly manic-depression are becoming increasingly recognized in violent youth (9). Youth convicted for homicide have a high incidence of psychotic thinking, paranoia, and auditory hallucinations ("hearing voices"). With histories of severe abuse and neglect, one should consider the possibility of a dissociative disorder (a disorder characterized by impairment of memory and consciousness under circumstances of severe stress and trauma). Alcohol or drug use surveys have found as many as 40% to 60% of juveniles arrested have substances in their system (45). Clues to these illnesses and behaviors are often present in families and children before adolescence, providing an earlier opportunity for intervention.

Implications:

1. Tremendous stigma exists for mental illness. However, much later suffering and harm can come to these youth. Hence, honest and open discussion is necessary to make informed decisions about assessment and treatment.

2. Education is key both for the child and family. Read, discuss, seek help, and have discussions with self-help agencies and information sources. All of these can be valuable in making informed decisions about children with mental health difficulties.

3. While there is some controversy about the prevalence of conditions such as adolescent manic-depression, violent youth often have one or more psychiatric conditions needing thorough assessment.

Limitations:

1. The research is fairly inconsistent about the prevalence of mental disorder in the community, and especially in children. This is due to changing and evolving definitions about disorders, different ways of measuring etc.

2. More people who do not suffer from mental illness commit crimes than those who do. Thus, one should definitely not conclude that mental illness generally causes criminal behavior.

3. The role of mental illness in crime is highly debatable with regards to how the legal system views guilt. Having a mental illness in and of itself doesn't necessarily mean the disorder is related to any crime that was committed.

D4. Serotonin

Serotonin is a very important neurotransmitter in the brain that helps send messages between nerve cells. It has been implicated even more than noradrenaline or dopamine in mechanisms involving violent behavior. Serotonin became famous when Prozac was introduced in the late 1980s. This and related medications work by blocking removal of serotonin from nerve cells, likely resulting in increased serotonin to do its work in the brain. Serotonin pathways are involved in many things, including regulation of impulses that could lead to aggression. Low levels of serotonin–related molecules have been found in people suffering from depression, criminals who are violent and impulsive, and those who attempted suicide by violent means (46). Serotonin is thought to be released by such things as physical contact, affection, and achieving positive status or high regard from others (47). It is thought to be one of the chief chemicals involved in the ability to stop and think, as well as mediate between the brain and the environment.

Implications:

1. Physical affection, emotional warmth, positive regard and reinforcement to children may actually influence the serotonin pathways in

the brain, improving their ability to handle stress, and decreasing their predisposition to violence.

2. As the biological sciences learn more knowledge about how we function, we may actually be able to offer better treatments to people who have impulse difficulties based on their serotonin physiology.

3. Serotonin has taught us that the environment does influence the brain and vice versa. Aside from affection, teaching children to reflect on their behaviors may change their brain structure and function. Hence, they should be able to learn to more automatically check their own aggressive impulses over time with practice.

Limitations:

1. Our knowledge of serotonin pathways in the brain is in its infancy. We will learn more as neuroimaging studies such as PET scans or functional MRI studies are performed. Theories will likely be modified accordingly.

2. Variations in level and function of serotonin are not specific to aggressive behavior and have been found in many psychiatric conditions.

3. While contemporary antidepressants that work in the serotonin world are more specific to that system, it has not yet been found that they influence aggressive behavior as much as one would think or hope.

D5. Dopamine

Dopamine, another neurotransmitter involved in brain function, is short for "*d*ihydr*oxy*phenylethyl*amine*". Dopamine is already fairly well known for involvement in Parkinson's disease and Schizophrenia. This chemical is now felt to be heavily involved in how the brain interprets rewards and pleasure. It appears dopamine functioning and its pathways can be altered by victimization and chronic stress, possibly resulting in enduring perceptions of hostility in the world (47). The experiences of abuse and neglect, as well as a thinking pattern of misinterpreting hostility, can lead to violence. Dopamine assigns value to such things as eating when hungry and surviving when threatened, thus leading to behavioral choices. Importantly, it has been found that reinforcing social skills, particularly through rewards, praise and recognition, works through the dopamine pathways (48) and could alter brain function over the long term.

Implications:

1. Positive rewards and recognition for children's efforts in any sphere likely go a long way towards improving their dopamine pathway functioning; this may serve to influence and perhaps enhance the child's potential for a positive outlook for self, others, the environment and the future.

2. Enduring stress or victimization from abuse alters brain functioning with dopamine playing a major role. Such experiences likely produce long-lasting changes in how victims see the world, which is why Post Traumatic Stress Disorder can be so enduring.

3. Substances such as nicotine, cocaine and others directly stimulate the dopamine system, leading to continuous and pleasurable reinforcement. This can make addiction particularly challenging to reduce or stop altogether.

Limitations:

1. The exact mechanisms of reinforcement and reward have not been completely worked out. The above summary is an oversimplified framework for illustrating that experiences and the environment do affect the brain's function.

2. Most research has taken place in animals, with human research far lagging for ethical and practical reasons. Thus much of what is said is based on similarity in physiology between other species and us.

3. Once we can actually see the brain at work, using new neuroimaging technology, we'll be in a much better position to understand how dopamine, serotonin, norepinephrine and other neurotransmitters and hormones work together.

D6. Noradrenaline

Noradrenaline is also known as norepinephrine. This is the neurotransmitter involved in the infamous "fight or flight" response. Threats, stress, and aversive experiences all tend to increase noradrenaline activity in the brain. This increase in the level of arousal leads to increased vigilance in the individual and defensive reactions to people or events (which may lead to aggression). Research has found higher levels of noradrenaline in military personnel having a more substantial history of aggressive behavior (49). This finding has also been replicated in violent offenders in state psychiatric hospitals (50). In an application of these findings, the drug propanolol has been sometimes found to be useful in aggression (51). It acts by blocking the action of noradrenaline in the brain, particularly in individuals with neurological damage, to reduce violent or explosive behavior.

Implications:

1. Chronic threat, fear, and terror can alter norepinephrine physiology in the brain. This in turn can lead to increased vigilance and expectation of aggression from others. An individual can be more predisposed to aggressive acts under these circumstances if survival is in danger.

2. It may be possible in the future to tailor medications to one's neurotransmitter systems in order to alleviate such heightened arousal levels and keep one's functioning more optimal.

3. Protection of children from adverse experiences such as abuse, violence, bullying and other threats can likely help to keep their emotional and neurotransmitter systems from shifting into overdrive.

Limitations:

1. We have discussed but three neurotransmitters. There are estimates of between 50 and 100 chemicals that act within the brain. Thus the picture is far from the simplistic description offered thus far.

2. How the known brain chemicals interact is being actively investigated. For example, we know that noradrenaline can influence dopamine functioning.

3. Reports about levels of noradrenaline in aggressive people have been inconsistent. For example, decreases in levels of noradrenaline have also been found in violent offenders. Further, propanolol is not always effective in decreasing aggression.

D7. Genetic influences

The relative roles of nature (genetics) and nurture have always been debated. Most current researchers suggest that an interaction between the two leads to behavior. Research evidence implies that general antisocial behavior may be more influenced by genetic mechanisms than violent behavior. One reason for this is that violence generally occurs within a pattern of more generally deviant behavior. There is some evidence of individuals in some families sharing certain personality traits such as novelty or thrill seeking (52). Also, more attention is being focussed on the neurotransmitter pathways previously discussed, to seek if certain genes involving specific dopamine, serotonin or norepinephrine receptors are more common in some families. There is even a specific syndrome (Brunner's syndrome) in a Dutch family involving a change in a serotonin related enzyme leading to increased aggression (53).

Implications:

1. There is strong evidence for susceptibility to alcoholism and substance abuse being transmitted genetically within certain families. Application of this may aid early violence prevention efforts.

2. There is emerging data about sensation seeking personality traits, and antisocial/criminal behavior in general being more common in certain families. Opportunities may thus exist in future for detection and interruption of these cycles.

3. As genes and environment do interact, the more supportive, nurturing, consistent, and rewarding the parenting and home environment, the more likely genetic contributions to antisocial behavior will be minimized.

Limitations:

1. We know very little about the mechanism by which genes may influence aspects of antisocial behavior.

2. Studies finding family linkages are to be interpreted cautiously due to potentially smaller and more diverse study samples in North American culture. Many genetic studies are done in more homogeneous (e.g. European) countries.

3. We know so little about so few genes now that any conclusions about their role are tentative at best. This will very likely change in the future.

D8. Delivery complications

In one particular study that looked at the interaction between biological and social factors, having complications at birth, when coupled with early rejection as a baby by the caregiver significantly increased one's likelihood of violence in later life (54). Examples of delivery problems included forceps extraction, breech delivery, umbilical cord problems and long duration of birth. Only when one or more of these were added to the following factors did the increased risk occur: attempts to abort the fetus, unwanted pregnancy, and placement of the infant into full-time institutional care for over 4 months of the first year of life. The resulting 4.5% of men who had both situations (rejection and birth problems) accounted for 18% of all of the crimes committed by persons in the study. This study is one of the very few to look at the complexity of interactions that can lead to violent behavior later in life.

Implications:

1. Birth complications usually do not increase the risk of violence when combined with a non-rejecting home environment. Thus supports to caregivers need to be in place to decrease the chance of early rejection.

2. Continued public health education and individual birth control efforts will prevent unwanted pregnancy. This by implication should decrease the rate of births of potentially violent men in the future.

3. Increasing caregiving skills and support to new parents may help in reducing the potential for parental rejection.

Limitations:

1. These results were found in Europe and would need replication in North America. The more heterogeneous nature of our society, and the higher crime rate may lead to different results.

2. These findings do not suggest that birth complications and early caregiver rejection actually lead to violent behavior. Thus the mechanism of this finding is still elusive.

3. There are many other influential risk factors that could change the course of a child's development. For example, 82% of the crimes were done by individuals who did not possess both factors.

D9. Small babies

Low birth weight and SGA (small for gestational/pregnancy age) babies have also been found to be more at risk for violent behavior later in life (55). However, as with the previous study, the effect of stress in the home environment has been found to greatly influence their risk. In one study, families that suffered from social disruptions were particularly hazardous for these babies; such situations include separation of the baby from the mother, marital conflict, an absent father, "illegitimacy" of the child, or parental mental health problems (56). While it is unclear how these babies are at more risk for violence and antisocial behavior later on, they are known to suffer a very high rate of neurological problems, which may predispose them to violent behavior (57). Thus having a premature baby in and of itself is likely not much of a risk factor unless there is a disruptive home environment.

Implications:

1. Small, possibly neurologically challenged babies can be very stressful and difficult for parents early on. A great deal of medical, mental health, and family support is required to sustain one's efforts and energies through this time.

2. Early prevention would include ensuring a stable home environment, readiness for a newborn (as much as feasible), and an available part-

ner or other social supports and resources. This would minimize any adverse social effects on the baby, especially if small or premature.

3. As with delivery complications, one should strive to ensure that social risk factors (separation, conflict etc.) are minimized as much as possible to increase the likelihood of a healthy baby and good social development. Otherwise the parent, child and society could suffer.

Limitations:

1. Some of the work that has found these results has used small numbers of people in the studies. Thus results are fairly tentative at this point, until larger studies replicate the findings.

2. As noted, the mechanisms of small or low birth-weight babies being at increased risk of aggression are not well understood. There is some support for neurological vulnerability, but this needs further testing.

3. The relative contributions of biological and social factors are difficult to tease out. Regardless, the best outcome involves a good home environment in spite of any biological risk factors.

D10. Nutrition

In the 1970s, there were reports of a link between a high dietary sugar intake and aggressive and hyperactive behavior. One very interesting study of adolescents involved juvenile delinquents within the youth prison system. 276 male delinquents were given new diets of complex carbohydrates (breads, pasta, vegetables, cereal etc.) An average 25% reduction in the frequency of rule violations was found for each individual on this diet which replaced simple sugars and food additives. Further, this finding was subsequently replicated in nine juvenile detention centers across the United States (58). It should be noted that hypoglycemia, or low blood sugar, can also lead to aggression and irritability. Although it is far from clear why better diet should influence aggressive behavior, likely mechanisms may include influencing hormone levels or as yet poorly understood brain function.

Implications:

1. A good nutritious diet has many beneficial effects on health. It is thus possible that good nutrition also influences behavior and should be considered important in any event as children grow.

2. Regulation of sugar intake, including switching from simple sugars to more complex carbohydrates will help optimize sugar in the body.

3. Alcohol abuse also lowers sugar to possibly hypoglycemic (low blood sugar) levels and this may be one mechanism of increased aggression with alcohol consumption.

Limitations:

1. In the above studies, other institutional changes likely contributed to the observed decrease in behavioral disruption. These may have included counseling, addition of females to the facilities etc.

2. Individual behavior often improves anyway during the course of admission to penal institutions or very structured settings. Thus whether the improved behavior was only due to diet is debatable.

3. More must be known about the relationship between sugar, hormones, neurotransmitters, brain function and behavior before conclusions can be drawn about the nature of the influence of diet on behavior.

E1. Exposure to violence

Young children, as well as adolescents, are at increased risk if they live in homes or communities with heavy exposure to chronic violence (59). Some of these children develop symptoms similar to those described in Post

Traumatic Stress Disorder (60). These include the following: retreating inward from the external world and environment, experiencing anxiety, anger, violence, nightmares, having fewer interests, detaching from others, suffering from a constricted range of emotions and avoiding many situations that could re-ignite their anxious and terrifying feelings. Many people cover up these feelings with a false bravado, acting uncaringly with little empathy for others. They generally become more and more desensitized to the world around them and cut off from their feelings in particular. As we saw earlier, more and more crimes are being committed in an emotionally detached manner. Exposure to violence may thus be contributory.

Implications:

1. Efforts to remove children from violent environments and households may assist in decreasing the damage from anxiety, anger, and emotional detachment.

2. Many are concerned about the level of violence in the media. However, the literature suggests that that this kind of exposure is particularly damaging to vulnerable children, such as those already desensitized.

3. Although absent fathers is also a risk factor, when both partners are present, the potential contribution of both of their levels of aggression and empathy need to be considered. Parents who themselves have low empathy and are aggressive need a lot of support and parenting skills to protect their young from themselves.

Limitations:

1. We need to know more about the characteristics of adults who are abusive or have other characteristics that expose children to violence both in and outside the home.

2. More studies with larger sample sizes of participants need to be done to try to work out the mechanisms associated with children exposed to violence.

3. The role of genetic contributions may overlap considerably with family violence when one considers that violence can be repeated between generations. Thus we need studies that combine these two and other risk factors together.

E2. Violence in the media

Movies, music videos, video games, violence in the news and on television, and the Internet have all added to the public's concern about the effects of media violence on today's children. Massive scientific literature over the last few decades generally comes to the conclusion that indeed exposure to media violence does contribute to the development of violent behavior (61). Various mechanisms and theories have been proposed. Important influences on children seem to be learning aggressive attitudes, believing that violence is justified and solves problems, heightened hostility and sensitivity to perceived threats from others, and desensitization of feelings and emotions (62, 63). Also violence in the media may increase a child's stimulation and arousal level in the short term, which may lead to aggressive acting out of the observed behavior. Despite all of this data, children most at risk seem to be those who already live in violent environments, where violence is the norm in the home or community, and where there is little attempt to moderate the effects of the observed violence.

Implications:

1. Violence in the media is but one factor, albeit an important one, that contributes to violence in children at risk. It likely is additive to other risks in vulnerable children.

2. If children are already at risk due to family or neighborhood factors, limiting viewing or discussing the effects of what children see may

help them digest socially appropriate non-violent norms even if they see it in the media.

3. The younger the child, the less cognitive ability they may have to moderate the influence of observed violence (i.e. as being unrealistic or unethical).

Limitations:

1. Although boys tend to watch more violent media than girls, research indicates that they may both be affected and influenced equally from this exposure (64). How much exposure is required is unknown.

2. Most children and youth who observe violence in the media are not themselves violent. Hence, children who are already vulnerable are the most worrisome group.

3. The relationship between observing media violence and aggression in the child is not simple. More needs to be known about how it influences a child's thinking and behavior, as well as how to protect them against the effects of inevitable viewing.

F1. Anxiety

Anxiety is one symptom within a group known as "internalizing" symptoms. These include worrying, nervousness, as well as anxiety. Depression is another internalizing type of symptom. In large studies over time, the presence of anxiety fortunately has been not been found to be linked with violent behavior in adolescence. In fact, some researchers have found that anxiety can be protective, although only mildly, against development of violence later on (65). It is not clear why this is so. Perhaps, children who worry more think about future consequences for behavior; they may be more prone to guilt, or they may suffer more emotional pain from the anxiety and worrying, thus inhibiting their aggressive behavior. Although it may be protective against violence, people with anxiety may suffer tremendously from post traumatic stress problems, phobias, or obsessive-compulsive symptoms.

Implications:

1. Children who are highly prone to anxiety or worry are likely at low risk for violent behavior. It is not as clear if this risk is still low when it comes to antisocial behavior in general.

2. How to interpret the total absence of anxiety is unclear. However, some people believe that such adjectives as callousness, emotional detachment, and lack of empathy may capture the opposite of anxiety. This was previously discussed under section B6, "Lack of empathy".

3. Children who have behavioral problems may exhibit "fearlessness". This is essentially lack of anxiety about consequences to the point of dangerousness. Such children exhibit risky, often impulsive behavior. Learning about consequences to self and others of such behaviors may cultivate a healthy respect for reasonable boundaries of behavior.

Limitations:

1. Some researchers have found that youth with antisocial behavior are actually at increased risk for development of anxiety and depressive disorders (66). Discrepancies may have to do with how the studies were conducted, what was measured, and whether symptoms or disorders were the focus.

2. Anxiety is by itself but one mildly protective factor. If youth have many other risk factors, these could obliterate any protective effects of the anxiety.

3. The knowledge of "anxiety" being protective is difficult to use proactively. However, thinking about consequences of behavior is always a valuable way to enhance mature development.

F2. Social skills

Having socially desirable skills has been shown to be quite protective against future violent behavior in children. Children who are aggressive can misperceive others' social or nonverbal cues and believe they are being challenged, verbally attacked, or "dissed" as it is called, even when this isn't the case. One of the most promising therapies for aggressive children is social skills training (67). Such skills include appropriate use of free time, sense of humor, ability to compromise, accepting constructive criticism, initiating conversation, listening skills, accepting not getting one's own way, avoiding fights, ignoring taunts and teasing, as well as attending to assigned tasks such as homework as directed (68). Ultimately if everyone including adults mastered these skills, which can be taught and learned, opportunities and frequencies of violence would likely diminish.

Implications:

1. Aggressive children can benefit from therapeutic social skills groups. However, such skills need to be practiced at home, school, and with peers, for mastery much like any other competency.

2. Teaching children prosocial ways to deal with peers and adversity should empower children. They will learn other ways to master themselves and influence others that do not promote violence.

3. Social skills learned when young should carry over to adolescent and adult relationships, workplace situations and interpersonal dealings in general.

Limitations:

1. There are times when children do face realistic threat and aggression from others. Social skills by themselves are useful but may not protect them if the danger of violence is real.

2. Social graces are notable in a society that seems to emphasize individual self-absorption and gratification. Thus it can be difficult to maintain a civilized demeanor when those around you appear to lack social skills, courtesies and pleasantries.

3. Social skills by themselves may not be sufficient therapy for aggressive children. These children suffer from many other risk factors that need to be addressed in order impact their day to day lives. Parenting and family focussed interventions are additionally valuable.

F3. Goal setting

The ability to set short and long terms goals is an important part of many interventions for aggressive children (68). Goal setting is one potential way to help solve problems and achieve in life. Many youth are quite aimless in their approach to their lives; they drift along without direction, waiting for good and bad things to happen to them, or have often just lost interest and motivation. The ability and skill involved in setting personal goals can is related to the concept of "Self-directedness", a positive personality trait (69). Youth with antisocial personalities and behaviors can hopefully mature and become more self-directed over time. Thus many youth have the potential to "outgrow" their antisocial ways. However, a lot of damage to themselves, families and others gets done along the way. Attempting to instill goal setting and a sense of control over one's destiny can help children have better (but hopefully not too much) self-esteem and sense of accomplishment.

Implications:

1. Children should be taught to set short-term goals that are easily achievable. The emerging satisfaction and achievement will enable them to set longer-term goals and sustain their efforts.

2. Modeling may be useful here. Children who witness their parents setting and achieving their goals, as well as dealing with adversity as it arises will learn a great deal.

3. Children tend to have short attention spans around setting personal goals and directing their own lives (to the extent possible). Thus keeping the exercise fun and rewarding them for reaching their own goals can be excellent reinforcement.

Limitations:

1. Goal setting is but one focus of much larger initiatives in violence prevention. However, everything little thing can contribute, especially if skills learned are transferable to other life situations.

2. Even though long range studies have found that antisocial personality is primarily a problem in young men that can improve with time, one should not wait that long to establish personal goal setting as an important priority. Such an important skill is best learned when young and practiced to achieve repeated success.

3. People who are successful criminals can also set goals, just those of which society disapproves. Thus it is important to make goals achievable, as well as morally useful.

F4. Vocational training

The purpose of employment and vocational training programs in the juvenile justice system is to engage youth in gainful employment, give them a sense of achievement, provide some income, as well as hope and motivation to finish their own education. Certain programs such as Job Corps or JOBSTART have been evaluated (70,71). With respect to Job Corps, participants were five times more likely to earn a high school diploma compared to other youth. JOBSTART youth more often achieved their high school diploma as well, and at the end of one year had lower rates of re-arrest than other out-of-school youth. The programs involved various combinations of job skills, family support, and remedial academic skills. Other studies of vocational training programs, when evaluated, unfortunately have not consistently found that replacing school work with training to be as promising in violence prevention over the long term (72).

Implications:

1. For youth who have been truant, unmotivated, or failing the education system, some of them may benefit from vocational training in well-organized and comprehensive programs.

2. Some youth have talents and skills technically that may not show up in academic testing or the education system. Thus it is possible they will flourish more in the work force if given the chance and supported.

3. For vocational training to work, support for things such as transportation, child care, guidance, mentoring, and counseling may all be necessary.

Limitations:

1. It is not really clear who ultimately benefits from vocational training, as many studies have not found beneficial effects when groups of participants were evaluated.

2. Most program evaluations have unfortunately found that any protective or violence prevention effects were lost after the first year or so of some studies.

3. Youth are not always assigned randomly to these studies; thus it is unclear if results are due to this bias in program selection or actually due to the effects of the program.

F5. Religious activity

People who participate in religious activities have actually been found to be less likely to have antisocial personality traits (73). They apparently also have fewer impulsive personality features. Religious activity doesn't necessarily mean attending church on a regular basis or involvement in organized religion. In people for whom some religious belief and practice plays a role in their lives, the religious activity may act as a protective force against the development of antisocial activity, including violence. Interesting, religious activity not only serves as a protective factor that serves to decrease the violence potential, but also has been found to diminish suicide risk (74). Religious activity may serve many functions in this regard. A sense of community, reinforcement of family practices and togetherness, belief in a higher power and broader destiny, source of strength, and a prosocial belief system may all be playing a role.

Implications:

1. Fewer people these days may be attending church. The above findings give one pause to think if our fragmented and isolated society is missing an important bonding and social mechanism.

2. The modern Christian movement has increased its participant numbers. Perhaps the community, social as well as religious beliefs therein appeal to those who feel society has lost its values.

3. It is likely that families would have to participate as a whole to reinforce the protective aspects of religious activity and practice. Otherwise the lack of reinforcement could lead to loss of protective effect.

Limitations:

1. Most of the studies have been with adults. Thus The implications for violence and suicide prevention in childhood and youth are less clear.

2. It is not clear if and how religious activity actually protects against violence. Larger, better-designed studies on protective factors may help with these questions.

3. Around 10% of those with adult antisocial personality are affiliated with a church. Also, many if not most people who do not attend church are not themselves violent.

F6. Immunization

Childhood immunization is rather routine in our society. However, from a prevention point of view, regular follow through of children's immunization schedules does contribute to a lower potential for violent behavior. This is because many infectious diseases subsequently lead to brain damage, which we have seen is a risk factor for later crime, violence, and substance abuse. The relevant illnesses for which vaccinations routinely exist include measles, mumps, rubella, poliomyelitis, diphtheria, pertussis (Whooping cough), tetanus, meningitis, and hepatitis B (75). Most and hopefully all children get routine screens and medical appointments as well as their "shots". From a public health perspective, efforts to educate new parents about the need for keeping vaccination appointments are very worthwhile. Likely children most at risk have other medical and social risk factors that interfere with proper medical follow-up if this is problematic.

Implications:

1. All new parents need to know the schedules for proper immunization of their children. This is usually well documented and reinforced by the medical and nursing practitioners.
2. Children at risk may have parents who are less educated or more stressed; hence they may need extra attention, reminders, and supports to ensure follow-through with appointments actually occurs.
3. Children who already suffer from some sort of brain or neurological injury or problem are likely at increased risk.

Limitations:

None known.

CHAPTER TWO: FACTORS RELATED TO THE PARENT(S)

Risk Factors
Protective Parental Factors

A1. Early marriage

Adolescence is these days a fairly complex and demanding time. The pressures from family, friends, school, partners, and society are tremendous. The urge to settle into some perceived stability such as marriage is enticing to some. This is seen as the answer to many problems—dating, love, parents, poor self-esteem, to name a few. Unfortunately, it is usually not that simple. Early marriage, especially in adolescence, has actually been found to generally increase economic problems for women in particular (76). One reason for this is that these women tend to not complete their education and then become emotionally and financially dependent on their husbands. Such situations have been linked with marital breakdown, spousal violence, child abuse and neglect, and later violence in the children of such marriages (77). These are very good reasons for getting one's own life in order before settling down in a relationship, especially when children are potentially involved.

Implications:

1. Women and men should generally delay marriage until beyond adolescence. The outcomes for violence prevention, economic security, and children's health would be improved.

2. While one does try to separate from one's family of origin somewhat in adolescence, switching into or starting one's own family isn't necessarily the answer to one's problems or future.

3. Finishing school first to provide for a better future will likely increase opportunities, potential achievements, independence and hopefully add more variety to one's life than marrying when young.

Limitations:

1. In the "good old days" many women married very young and many achieved stable marriages; certainly not all of these couples produced violent children.

2. Many couples who married early were "childhood sweethearts". This romantic notion isn't always unfounded, although it is difficult to predict if and when marriages will be successful.

3. The link with having violent children is much stronger for unmarried, uneducated mothers than those who simply married young.

A2. Early pregnancy

Some adolescent girls, especially those who are marginalized or estranged from their families or society, may feel that having a baby will give them someone to love and someone to love them back. This may be true in an ideal world but is not the full picture in reality. An early (adolescent) onset of pregnancy and parenthood has been linked to increased violence for both the female parent and the resultant child. This is particularly true if the pregnancy happens before marriage or before onset of a stable intimate relationship. As we saw from the last section, relationships and marriage can initially look stable but may not pan out over time. Some of the reasons that may explain the increased risk of violence include economic hardship, lack of skills and education, lack of opportunity, and last but not least, the joyful yet incredibly daunting and challenging task of successfully raising children.

Implications:

1. Having a child should not be an easy decision. The financial, emotional, and physical commitment lasts for decades. Thus careful thought about the future should guide the decision to have children at any age.

2. The highest risk children tend to be born in families that involve young, impoverished, isolated women with low educational achievement (78). Such parents can then become depressed, stressed, angry, frustrated or neglectful parents when they realize how challenging a job being a parent really is.

3. The phrase "it takes a village" to raise a child can be quite accurate. Children, especially active or temperamental ones, need multiple supports and caregivers to give the primary parent(s) relief. Adolescents may not yet have sufficient social and emotional support, as well as stable enough lives, to effectively raise children.

Limitations:

1. Not all children born to young, single mothers turn out to be violent. However, generally in these cases, protective factors such as easy temperament, social support, or superior parenting skills likely exist.

2. Unwanted or unexpected children can still grow up to be fine citizens if loved, parented, and nurtured by either their primary parent(s) or adoptive ones.

3. While pregnancy prior to marriage increases risk, pregnancy during marriage doesn't guarantee anything either. Most things are

contextual. If enough protective factors exist in either case, the odds of raising violent children will be lessened.

A3. Low education level

Low education level and achievement in parents are consistently in studies found to be risk factors for aggression, violence, and antisocial behavior in their children (78). Not that this is a universal truth, but in high-risk families, poor education adds another important layer of risk. In fact, as mentioned previously, young high school dropouts who have children early tend to be the most vulnerable parents in our society. They are likely under-skilled in today's competitive job market, have few financial resources, are developing but have not yet achieved full emotional maturity, and are often socially isolated; hence, their readiness for children is questionable. It is also possible that many also don't support their children's educational efforts, as they themselves have not had good experiences and success in the school system. In any event, this is one finding that is very robust—the higher the level of educational achievement by a parent, the less likelihood of violence in the child.

Implications:

1. Young people should strive as much as possible to complete at least their high school education before embarking on early marriage and child-rearing. Completing school does them and their eventual children a big favor.

2. If children are already in the picture, even though it is more difficult it would behoove any parent to finish their education in order to protect them and their children from further financial and emotional stress.

3. Finishing education is good for one's self-esteem and good modeling for children. Such prosocial activities lessen children's risk of behavioral problems.

Limitations:

1. Not every poorly or uneducated parent has an aggressive child. Other stresses and risk factors likely have to accumulate to really worsen the child's outlook (79).

2. It is easier said than done to finish schooling. Such issues as motivation, learning problems, high standards, and level of support can make it very tough to complete and apply an education.

3. The education system is undergoing tremendous change as labor, economics, and society changes. This can be quite bewildering to those who are re-entering or completing degrees or diplomas.

A4. Alcohol use in pregnancy

Using alcohol during pregnancy has many detrimental side effects. Alcohol does get to the fetus and is particularly damaging in the first 12 weeks, when the fetus' brain and nervous system are starting to develop. Effects of fetal alcohol exposure have been recently become more commonly known. They include physical signs of immaturity at birth, as well as psychiatric problems such as attention difficulties, anger, aggression, violence, learning problems, problems with impulse control, and hyperactivity (80). Also, alcohol use can be transmitted either genetically and/or through modeling to children who later become addicted. Thus pregnancy is an optimal time to cut back, stop, and/or get treatment. This will hugely benefit the mother, child, their relationship, and society through a decrease in the emotional and financial costs associated with alcohol consumption.

Implications:

1. In terms of violence prevention, alcohol abuse or dependence should be ideally treated or stopped prior to pregnancy. Then one can be surer of not exposing the fetus to any toxic effects.

2. Once pregnancy becomes known, addressing alcohol use is still imperative as one can still prevent a lot of later damage. However, as stated the first 12 weeks of pregnancy are the most crucial for the fetus.

3. Alcohol is often be used to excess in social surroundings, families, and relationships. One must seriously look at one's environment to measure whether a child will be exposed to a wholesome, nurturing, and healthy atmosphere.

Limitations:

1. "Harm reduction" is one model of alcohol treatment in which moderation and minimizing damage is more the goal than total abstinence. Unfortunately, we don't really know the safest lower limit of alcohol use during pregnancy (other than none).

2. One needs a great deal of support to decrease or stop one's consumption of alcohol and substances. This can be difficult if the people in one's life are also using and abusing.

3. There are an insufficient number of treatment programs for alcohol and drug use. Thus the earlier one admits to a problem and gets on a waitlist, the better the potential outcome.

A5. Smoking in pregnancy

Up to 20% of women smoke at some point during their pregnancy. Most people are by now aware that smoking has many adverse health consequences. However, smoking during pregnancy has also been documented to be linked with a difficult temperament in babies (81). Cigarette use by pregnant women results in babies having more irritability, difficulty settling, difficulty in feeding and sleeping routines etc. Cognitive and learning problems have also been found in babies whose mothers smoked. Also, prematurity and low-birth weight babies could also result. Having newborns can be challenging at the best of times, but having an irritable, small, and temperamentally difficult baby, especially if in an atmosphere of stress, social isolation, conflict and poverty can really stretch one's patience and resilience. Thus, as much as possible, even stopping smoking for a few months during pregnancy would be helpful.

Implications:

1. All of the effects of smoking mentioned above—small size, difficult temperament, and learning problems have been linked with later violence in vulnerable children. Hence quitting cigarettes should really reduce this risk.

2. Given the fetus' vulnerability, even reducing or stopping just during pregnancy should cut down on future risk of violence and medical complications in babies.

3. There are more options now for quitting smoking. Physicians or public health nurses can suggest effective ways to help reduce cigarette use.

Limitations:

1. As with alcohol use, smoking can be a group experience. It takes support and willpower to quit, especially when those around you smoke.

2. One doesn't always know right away that one is pregnant. However, if sexually active and not using precautions, realistically a pregnancy

could easily occur. Smoking, drugs, and alcohol are very damaging at this time.

3. If we didn't do things that were bad for us, we probably wouldn't be human. Despite this temptation, successful reduction of cigarette use often inspires pursuit of other goals.

A6. Prenatal (before birth) nutrition

Poor diet and nutrition during pregnancy have been linked, in the presence of other risk factors, to a long-term increased risk of antisocial behavior and violence in the children (82). It is likely that such factors, which include insufficient calories, low or no intake of iron or folate, unbalanced diet, and drug or alcohol intake can operate collectively in some people to increase risk for resultant babies and children. Another such "prenatal" factor includes exposure to toxins (83) such as lead or cadmium (cadmium is found in cigarette smoke, contaminated water, and is high in shellfish and liver). In any event, poor maternal nutrition has been linked to early and prolonged onset of oppositional, aggressive, and antisocial behavior, especially when combined with other risk factors in the mother, family, community or society.

Implications:

1. Nutritional advice and counseling can be quite valuable for new mothers. This is particularly true in high-risk situations where social supports are low and/or drug and substance use exists.

2. Pregnancy is a good place to start having healthier habits such as a balanced diet, paying attention to vitamins, minerals, sugar, and calories. Habits gained during this period of time may be carried forward in subsequent years.

3. Good nutrition in pregnancy hopefully is a prelude to good nutrition for children. They need wholesome meals and non-toxic environments to learn and grow.

Limitations:

1. It is not clear how or if poor prenatal nutrition itself directly leads to antisocial behavior in children. Likely other influences need be present.

2. Poverty is a major limiting factor in the diets of children and families. More and more families are below the poverty line and this has direct relevance to their ability to properly feed their children and themselves.

3. Because it is so difficult to separate out prenatal factors and influences, consultation from dieticians, public health, and physicians is crucial to ensure a good start for any baby.

A7. Poor Prenatal Care

All fetuses, if they are to make it to the end of pregnancy in a healthy manner, need good "prenatal" (before birth) care. We have already identified some of the early risk factors—smoking, drug and alcohol use, and poor nutrition but there are others. Babies who are born prematurely, who have low birth weight or very small size are at higher risk for medical and neurological complications. These issues can often be detected early with proper medical and nursing monitoring over the course of pregnancy. Further, current standards for prenatal care include education about the emotional and physiological changes associated with pregnancy, childbirth and infancy, fetal growth and development, and support (84). Nowhere are these steps more vital than in high-risk pregnancies (those with potential medical problems or where social supports and educational achievement are low) to prevent later onset of violence and behavioral problems in the children.

Implications:

1. Routine and regular appointments during the course of any pregnancy are very preventive steps, both for the child and the mother. Medical, neurological, and psychological problems can then be detected and helped early before they progress.

2. Although it is often difficult to admit or accept that help and support are needed, in this situation they are vital to the health and future welfare of all parties, especially the baby.

3. In particular, home visits by public health nurses and professionals (see next section) has been found to play a vital, early, and effective role in preventing onset and severity of later behavioral problems in high risk children.

Limitations:

1. One of the key ingredients is a healthy and therapeutic relationship between the mother and health care professional. Women should feel comfortable in trusting and talking to their caregivers, doctors, nurses, and support staff; understandably this isn't always easy.

2. Funding problems are limiting effective prevention services to newly pregnant women and mothers. It is paradoxical that such cost effective measures as prenatal care are vulnerable to budget cuts.

3. Sometimes women don't actually realize that they are pregnant and valuable time is then lost. Thus being vigilant to this potential, using proper contraceptive precautions if pregnancy is not desired, and having support from partners also play a huge protective role.

A8. Low parental involvement

Degree of parental involvement in children's lives appears to be a critical factor in increasing or reducing the risk of violent behavior in youth. Quantity and quality of communication between parent and child are very important. If there is little conversation, one won't know what the child is doing, thinking and feeling. It has been found that the lower the communication and involvement in the child's life generally, the higher the amount of violent behavior by adolescence (85). Engaging in leisure activities with children has also been found to protect against future violence. This is particularly true of involvement of fathers with their sons' activities (5). As we have seen, involvement in children's education and schools is also protective. It is true that as children grow they separate from their parents and associate more with their peers; however, staying involved throughout adolescence is vital to keeping youth healthy.

Implications:

1. Fathers with male children in particular can contribute greatly to their son's development and mature behavior by participating in their extracurricular and leisure activities.

2. Making time to do even simple things with children can pay off huge dividends over time, both in terms of proper behavior, but also in the improved quality of adult-child relationships.

3. Talking to children as often and openly as possible about what they are doing, learning, thinking, and experiencing is highly recommended. Childhood is not a stress-free experience and children have few opportunities to reflect their ideas and worries with knowledgeable, experienced, and interested adults.

Limitations:

1. The relationship between involvement and violent behavior is stronger for boys than girls. While we don't know why, some factors may be girls' earlier maturation and development of interpersonal relationships outside the family.

2. There are only 24 hours in the day. Once work and chores are done, often there is little time left to talk or do leisure activities with children. Rethinking one's family schedule to build these in is challenging but ultimately more rewarding.

3. Parental involvement is difficult when one parent isn't around and the other has to deal with everything. Thus building in extended family involvement (grandparents, aunts, uncles etc.) can also help ease the time pressures and increase adult involvement with children.

A9. Poor monitoring of children

A fairly consistent finding in research has been that children who are poorly monitored have an increased risk of delinquent behavior, particularly in adolescence (86). However, there is also some evidence that too much monitoring may also increase their risk (87). Nevertheless, it has been found that when monitoring and supervision of children increases, the rates of antisocial and aggressive behavior can be reduced. There are no universally agreed upon rules or suggestions yet as to how or how much to monitor children and adolescents. Further, even if parents wish and are able to effectively monitor their children's after school behavior, they frequently don't have adequate access to information such as timing of extracurricular events, whereabouts of friends etc. Youth may resist disclosing their whereabouts but often do appreciate parental involvement when needed.

Implications:

1. Many delinquent acts happen during the afternoon and early evening, when youth are unsupervised. Knowledge of their whereabouts at these times may decrease the risk of trouble.

2. Working out a system of communication between family, friends, and school may be helpful in understanding what children are up to in the afternoons and evenings.

3. Increasing bonding, involvement, and communication should increase trust, which should facilitate direct and open communication between children and parents as to their whereabouts and activities.

Limitations:

1. Parents are often powerless as other systemic players such as schools or friends may not effectively communicate and support monitoring by the youth's parents.

2. Many parents have to work long hours to economically survive. This can preclude full knowledge of children's whereabouts at all times.

3. Research has not yet suggested effective ways to monitor children. Thus parents often get the blame without being offered support or advice about effective practices.

A10. Physical discipline

How to discipline children effectively has been the subject of much debate. What is clearer are suggestions on how not to discipline children. It is fairly clear now that physically punishments, particularly when there is already a conflictual relationship between child and parent, actually may increase a child's risk of being violent themselves (88,89,90). This may be because the physical punishment (slapping, hitting, using belts etc.)

models aggressive behavior, teaches the child violent ways to solve conflicts and problems, and teaches that power and control are more important than resolving disputes. The problem of course is that parents often don't know what else to do with very resistant children. Other strategies may include natural consequences, logical consequences, time out, and withdrawal of parental attention, amongst others.

Implications:

1. Specific parenting strategies to use other than physical punishment are available and useful if utilized consistently and with other strategies such as involvement, monitoring, play, praise etc.

2. Becoming an effective disciplinarian is a skill that takes practice and guidance. As alternatives to spanking, many parenting centers offer strategies and readings which when used repeatedly produce positive results for parents and children.

3. Hostile, inconsistent and physically punitive parenting will cause more harm than good over the long term, both for the relationship with the child, and the child's future violence potential. So while spanking may temporarily stop children's behavior, it will increase the likelihood that you'll see the undesired acts again.

Limitations:

1. Many people speak of the "good old days" when one could use physical punishment with children. How the punishment gets interpreted (as unjustified or appropriate) probably is quite important; this determines whether the child will model the physically aggressive behavior.

2. While physical punishment is no longer considered effective in teaching children discipline, it is especially harmful when combined

with other risk factors such as marital conflict or poor bonding between parent and child, to name but two of many.

B1. Home visitation for new mothers

One of the interventions that has strong evidence of reduction of children's future violence risk is home visitation for new mothers (91). The classic study targeted an area in New York state that had a high rate of child abuse and poverty. It was felt that early intervention, before the child was age 2 carried the most potential for good effects. Many of the new mothers were teenage, unmarried women who were quite poor. One group received visitation by a nurse from pregnancy through to age 2. A comprehensive set of services was provided including help with the mother's health, advice on baby care, pregnancy prevention, finding work, family involvement, social and other community agency involvement. 15 years later it was found that the mothers who received the 2 years of visits exhibited less child abuse and neglect, fewer subsequent births, less social assistance, fewer arrests and less drug use. Similarly their children had fewer emergency visits, cognitive problems, arrests, and drug use.

Implications:

1. New mothers who are at risk need and can benefit from a comprehensive set of services that public health professionals have to offer. Such interventions are cost-effective ways of really reducing the child's future violence risk.

2. The earlier the intervention, the better the overall outcome for the child. As a child grows and accumulates more risk factors, it becomes much more difficult to effectively intervene and help a child from having antisocial behavior.

3. Young mothers would do well to allow nurses into their homes to help them with various aspects of their own and their baby's health and welfare. The financial and emotional savings are tremendous.

Limitations:

1. Many young people feel intimidated or threatened by professional involvement. Thus earning trust to allow someone into one's home for over 2 years may be challenging for some.

2. As previously mentioned, a comprehensive universal plan of home visitation would be ideal. However, such insight and planning may be difficult in an environment in which short-term gains and immediate financial savings are emphasized.

3. Although early nurse home visitation is valuable, these children and families continue to be at some risk. Thus continued support from family and community agencies may be needed to maintain the gains made.

B2. Parent/child bond

The quality of the relationship between a parent and child is extremely important. In particular, closeness, emotional warmth, parental approval (when appropriate), affection, respect, identification between child and parent (in which the child wants to be like the parent in terms of character and behavior), humor and many other ingredients support a positive relationship between children and parents (92). Having such a solid foundation helps weather other storms that arise such as behavior problems, discipline, punishment and conflict. The "emotional bank" that is built up can be drawn upon at times of stress. Children who lack this relationship and closeness with the parent tend to see punishment as unjustified and merely the way in which adults solve problems between people, or exert control and power. Therefore it becomes more likely that the youth or child would use punitive or aggressive means to achieve his or her own goals.

Implications:

1. Building a healthy parent/child relationship is achievable by such things as noticing and rewarding positive behavior, sharing experiences, humor, support, guidance and many other things children need.

2. Punishment can be more readily effective and understood by children if they already have a warm, solid relationship with their parent(s). They then may see discipline more as necessary than unjustified.

3. Building an "emotional bank" can be done through play. Many fun books are available on how to play with children to help them learn about things such as relationship and problem-solving skills.

Limitations:

1. Proper balance between warmth, closeness, and limit setting/discipline can be difficult to achieve. Seeing a child mental health professional or reading any excellent parenting book can help. There is unfortunately, no magic formula.

2. Many families today are stretched for time, money, and resources. It becomes very difficult but paradoxically even more necessary to make "quality time" for children to build the relationships with them.

3. Some research has not found that the quality of bonding between youth and families predicts later violent behavior. This may be due to different research and statistical analyses. However, at a minimum, it can only help to establish such a positive atmosphere; besides, it's usually much more pleasant than chronic conflict!

B3. Play

Learning how to play with children, especially starting in the early pre-school years, is an important part of any violence prevention program. It begins a good foundation that enhances parental involvement, bonding with one's child, and can be fun! Foundations built during play help weather the storms when adults have to be firm, set limits, give consequences and discipline children. Many experts suggest that play include allowing the child to lead, using imagination and pretend play, keeping expectations reasonable for the child's age, praising the child's creative efforts, and describing and commenting on the child's playful activities, amongst other techniques (93). In high risk families in particular, healthy and creative play can be a vital part of parenting and family activities that decrease disruptive and aggressive behaviors.

Implications:

1. There is no ultimately right or wrong way to play. However, the above techniques are commonly used when teaching play that allows the child to grow and develop at his or her own pace.

2. Play hopefully allows one to relax a bit, enjoy children, and take a timeout from the stresses of being an adult. It is a great way to build a healthy foundation, which can stay solid despite later stress or conflict.

3. Childcare workers or preschool teachers are excellent sources of information about how to play with children. It often feels awkward or unnatural at first, but should get easier and more rewarding as time goes on.

Limitations:

1. Play is best attempted as early as possible (such as in the preschool years). Although it is never too late, older children may not catch on

to the idea of playing with adults as readily if the practice wasn't already there.

2. Time is so precious now that often there is little time for play. However, it is a lot like saving money—little by little it grows, earns interest and eventually pays off.

3. Many people have difficulty with play, as it feels too childish. However, hopefully the privacy of the home permits adults to play at the child's level of development without embarrassment.

B4. Reading to your child

Reading books with children accomplishes many positive things simultaneously. First of all, it is a really great way to get involved with them, as well as increase the warmth, emotional connection, and bonding between adults and children. Many prevention programs offer a toy and/or book-lending library as support for parents and children. Of course, reading to them and encouraging their love and interest in books and writings enhances children's cognitive, educational and intellectual development; we have already seen that these abilities can be compromised in aggressive or disruptive children. Reading with children works especially well in conjunction with early childhood education or preschool initiatives which support parental efforts at parenting, play, and fostering academic growth in their children (94). Children's books also frequently contain life lessons such as sharing, problem solving, friendship and empathy, all of which are also protective factors against violence.

Implications:

1. Taking every opportunity to explore the world of books will pay off in numerous ways via building relationships with children, fostering

their development, and influencing their brain to decrease their risk of aggression.

2. Libraries and drop-in centers are great resources for borrowing high quality children's books. They are both fun and educational. A love of learning that enhances the child's academics can start in preschool.

3. Children also learn by modeling from parents. Thus, if parents are seen reading, children will interpret reading as healthy and desirable and be more motivated to do so.

Limitations:

1. Again, time limitations can impinge on the good intentions of parents. Play, parental involvement, and reading all require time commitments that can be difficult to maintain with today's pressures.

2. Many parents find reading children's books boring or difficult, sometimes due to their own reading problems or level of patience. Use of story time in libraries and childcare centers can be a useful alternative.

3. Some children find reading less stimulating than playing video or computer games. However, it is important to try to instill a quiet pleasure in reading so the child won't continuously expect and seek highly stimulating activities.

B5. Parenting training, courses or education

In all likelihood, we are not born effective parents. We learn largely by trial and error, instinct, and observing models from our own childhood. From a violence prevention perspective, it has been found that teaching parents effective parenting strategies, particularly with pre-adolescent children, does decrease their children's risk of antisocial behavior (33). A confusing number of books, experts, and programs exist. However, the ones that have the strongest evidence of being effective tend to emphasize 3 main components. First is building a healthy parent-child relationship (see previous discussion about bonding, play, reading etc.). Second, practical ways of implementing strategies such as praise, rewards, consequences, setting limits and time out are emphasized. Finally, helping parents with their own problem solving, emotions, communication and social supports is considered vital.

Implications:

1. The younger the child (especially preschool), the more effective one can use parenting strategies which will help decrease problems later.

2. Parents should not be afraid to ask for help, support or strategies. Parenting is tough and requires patience, consistency and endurance.

3. Effective parenting comprises real and important skills that can be taught and learned.

Limitations:

1. High stress levels in parents need to be addressed in parenting programs so that effective parenting strategies can be learned and practiced, otherwise stressed parents tend to benefit less.

2. The older the child, the less likely that parenting strategies by themselves will effectively change the course of antisocial behavior. Other issues such as school, social and problem-solving skills, as well as family problems need to be addressed as well.

3. Long-term effects of parenting programs that include the 3 components listed above are still being researched and thus not yet guaranteed positive results for all families.

B6. Positive reinforcement

Although normally thought of as one of many parenting skills (95), the role of positive reinforcement is extremely important and deserves special mention. Many interactions between children and parents, especially those involving adolescents, start out, evolve and maintain their negative and conflictual quality over time. These interactions can become power struggles, shouting matches, and ongoing sources of conflict. People in general pay more attention to negative or "wrong" behavior than positive efforts. Positive reinforcement is all about searching for, noticing, acknowledging, as well as verbally and tangibly rewarding children's positive behaviors. As small targets are achieved, more problematic behaviors can be tackled. If their positive efforts go unnoticed, children will often resort to more negative and defiant behaviors.

Implications:

1. When children do things quietly, comply with requests, do their homework or any such desirable behavior, it would be helpful for them to be acknowledged and at least verbally praised.

2. As children start to comply with even one behavior, then noticing and rewarding others can help reduce conflict, as children can't change all of their negative behaviors at once.

3. Parenting programs can teach effective and timely ways to modify children's behavior through noticing positive behavior. Thus positive reinforcement, like any other skill, will hopefully become more natural over time.

Limitations:

1. Although giving praise or reward may feel unnatural, we adults are no different—we are motivated by pleasure, kind words, money, and achievement no less than children.

2. When adults are stressed or in bad moods, they are less likely to be positive. Although time is limited, addressing underlying stress, or at least timing out themselves until they can focus more positively on children will help adults create a healthier environment.

3. Positive reinforcement by itself isn't usually sufficient by itself to curb children's disruptive behavior. However, it can make life more pleasant when used along with other parenting strategies.

B7. Supporting children's educational success

As we have seen, children's educational achievements may help protect them from developing disruptive or antisocial behavior (96). However, they can seldom do this by themselves. In addition to reading early to children, parents and adults can help their children academically by taking an interest in their children's education and schooling. Although one cannot always help children solve academic or homework problems, ensuring that homework is completed, attending parent/teacher meetings, and supporting teachers, principals, and schools in their efforts will go a long way towards helping children achieve. Many children with behavior problems also have learning problems. Working with the school is extremely important to remedy these issues.

Implications:

1. Schools want children to succeed. Thus, caregivers should try to take the teachers' and other school personnel's comments and concerns seriously and work with them to help children.

2. It is important to advocate for children if either the parent or the school thinks there is a blockage to learning, such as learning disability or Attention Deficit/Hyperactivity Disorder.

3. Children need to focus and behave appropriately in school if they are to learn. If children are having behavioral problems in the school, working with the school to problem-solve will be both academically helpful for the child as well as good role modeling.

Limitations:

1. Public schools are under increasing financial pressures, resulting in fewer educational resources, and are thus continuously criticized. They really need more support from parents and community.

2. As the same time, children who have identified learning and behavioral problems should be supported psychologically and educationally, not ostracized. Unfortunately, sometimes a child with behavioral problems gets labeled a "problem child".

3. It is difficult to not be defensive when the school says a child is either causing problems, or has behavioral problems. However, schools usually have justifiable reasons for identifying such issues.

B8. Prevention of pregnancy

In the United States, an estimated 57% of all pregnancies and as many as 80% of all teen pregnancies are unintended (97). As noted, risks to babies born to single teen parents include physical abuse, emotional abuse, poverty, educational underachievement, and erratic supervision—all of which increase risk of later violence in the children. Many public health programs currently exist to attempt to educate adolescents about the consequences of pregnancy. The ones that were most promising included those that involved both males and females (98). For example, enforcement of child support rules apparently helps reduce casual sex in men that can lead to unintended pregnancy. Those men who are required to provide economic support for their children appear to be more willing to consistently use contraception to prevent future conception. Thus both men and women need internal and external reinforcement to prevent early pregnancy and reduce violence risk in their children.

Implications:

1. Adolescent (and adult) males and females both need to assume responsibility for prevention of unwanted pregnancy. To reduce future risk of violence and abuse, the use of proper contraception should be enforced by both parties.

2. Jurisdictions in which child support guidelines are reinforced encourage more responsible behavior, particular among sexually active men. If this is an option, it should be pursued to benefit current and future children.

3. Public health nurses, doctors and other professionals are great sources of information around contraceptive devices and pregnancy prevention. Informed choices lead to empowerment.

Limitations:

1. Prevention of pregnancy is well worth the effort but easier said than done. To some extent it is human nature to "go with the moment" since we are sexual beings. However, thinking about consequences and prevention is better in the long term.

2. Unfortunately it can still be considered less masculine or macho to use precautions. However, it is also true that such irresponsible behavior is also considered immature and not adult-like.

3. We still need more long-term studies to understand how much impact on youth violence is gained by delaying pregnancy and childbirth. However, we cannot wait on those studies to take necessary precautions.

Chapter Three: Factors Involving The Family

Social Factors
Family Practices
Medical/Psychological Factors
Protective Familial Factors

A1. Number of family moves

Moving can be a good thing when the neighborhood, schools, job, or proximity to social support improves. However, frequently moving the family during a child's life has been linked with an increased risk of violence in later adolescence (99). This may be due to many issues: economic necessity and the stress therein (moving due to poverty), disrupting a child's bonds with friends (especially prosocial influences), altering a child's connection with his or her neighborhood (again resulting in a sense of having no or little connection), and in particular changing a child's educational environment. The latter may contribute to disruption of peer relationships, decreased educational interest and achievement, and difficulties fitting into the new school. Further, disconnected children may face increased risk of teasing, bullying or attachment to other isolated, unhappy or otherwise disenfranchised children.

Implications:
1. Although some moves are normal throughout a child's life, the more disruption there is, the harder it is for some children to adjust socially and educationally.

2. Keeping some prosocial connections to friends despite moves may be one way to lessen the blow for children who do not cope well with change.

3. Usually moving is a big but necessary step. Considering and addressing the effects on a child's life as a whole may help the child process the upset or trauma.

Limitations:

1. The research on family mobility is somewhat inconsistent. The effects on children of moving may vary with age, sex, and the presence of other supports and risk factors.

2. The disruptive effects could be merely short-lived for some children and the advantages of moving may greatly outweigh the risks.

3. Little research has focussed on the question of why moves may influence development or exacerbation of aggressive or violent behaviors in children.

A2. Social bonding/attachments

Social bonding refers to the presence of supportive, emotionally warm relationships that children should have with adults. These should preferably be within one's own family, but could be external as well. Children who have families that are isolated, have few friends, as well as limited contact with extended family or community are generally at higher risk. Even in these families if the child is having behavioral problems, the presence of a quality relationship with one adult could somewhat protect against the development of violence (100). When children have no one at all to turn to or support them, then they can potentially becoming quite alienated, angry, vengeful or punitive in their behavior. Just having an adult around may be insufficient by itself, as the relationship does need some emotional foundation. Otherwise, children often look elsewhere for support and connection.

Implications:

1. Children at risk for aggression need someone with whom to talk, relate, and assist in sorting out problems and worries, as well as give them relief from their stress.

2. If this is not possible within a family, then children or youth could develop a healthy relationship with an extended family member (e.g. grandparent, teacher, therapist, or mentor). This could be very useful in his or her healthy development.

3. Ideally, as previously mentioned, good quality relationships should start early in the child's life as they take time to cultivate. It can be more difficult to successfully reach out to a troubled teen than a younger child youth. However, the right connection can also greatly assist adolescents.

Limitations:

1. It can be difficult to know who to trust in today's world. Thus many parents can be rightly skeptical when a non-family adult becomes important to a child.

2. It is difficult for some families to develop warm internal relationships when they are struggling to survive and dealing with conflict, stress, and potentially such things as alcohol or drug problems.

3. Although it is possible, it is a fine art to balance nurturing a child with discipline. Children will test limits but they do want and need to feel loved and supported.

A3. Stress

A simple way of thinking about stress is dividing it into stressful events (acute stresses) and ongoing daily frustrations and hassles (chronic stresses of life). One large study that surveyed youth in the United States found that acute stresses (serious medical illness, unemployment, divorce, separation, or serious accident) were not generally associated with an increased risk of violent behavior in youth (101). However, other data would strongly suggest that when families are followed over time, ongoing stresses such as economic stress, family breakdown, isolation, possibly work stress and the resulting emotional strain may influence the degree of emotional warmth, affection, communication, and attention that parents and other adults can realistically give children (102). We have already seen that this decreased quality of child-adult interactions may predispose to aggressive and antisocial behavior.

Implications:

1. Life is much more stressful and chaotic these days than in the past. It is quite possible that children are bearing the brunt of societal stress in the quality of their home, school and community environments.

2. Adults should strive as much as possible to examine their own levels of stress, anxiety and depression and to seek help even if only to get a relatively objective opinion. The reduced parental stress can only benefit children.

3. The contributions of chronic work, home, and life stress toward disruptive family life and child behavior problems are likely under-recognized and under-appreciated. Parents are often blamed for poor parenting when they are themselves recipients of unfair and uncompassionate practices in the systems and structures around them.

Limitations:

1. It can be difficult to objectively quantify stress as people perceive stress in their own ways. Some people are more resilient than others.

2. Some studies are merely cross-sectional surveys. They often don't validate the data and follow people over time to see the cumulative effects of stressful events on people.

3. A great many studies have concluded that "poor parenting" practices are very instrumental in producing children who are violent. While that may be true to an extent, what studies don't do well is explain why there are poor parenting practices, and how to help adults who are under chronic stress to be better parents, caregivers, mentors etc.

A4. Economics

In the 1980s and 1990s there was an explosion of drug and gang related violence among American youth. However, many sociology researchers believe that non-youth factors were to blame. For example, the severe loss of traditional jobs in urban areas, sharp increases in unemployment and poverty in young men, decreases in opportunities for material, educational and vocational advancement, and increased economic inequality all have been linked with the increase in rates of homicide. Interestingly, it has also been found internationally that countries (such as Sweden, France, Germany, and Holland) which provide more generous social economic help, health care, family allowances, and other social benefits tend to have lower child poverty levels and lower levels of youth-related violence and homicide in particular (103). All of these social factors impinge on families as they struggle to survive in today's world.

Implications:

1. Serious thought at a policy level should be given to the effects of unemployment, poverty, and family deprivation on the national rates of violent offenses, particularly given slower economic growth.

2. Society as a whole needs a debate about whether the individualistic approach, as adopted in the United States, is beneficial for the way the less fortunate are treated.

3. The costs of the juvenile justice system dealing with youth (especially at tens to hundreds of thousands of dollars for incarceration, legal, police, judiciary, and probation services) compared to the costs of greater financial and health assistance to families would be interesting to compare.

Limitations:

1. Economic factors don't explain all violence but contribute to large trends. Other social factors will be discussed later, but include disorganization of previously strong societal structures (such as churches, neighborhoods, and extended families).

2. Some research is emerging that the highest risk youth are those who have both social factors (such as poverty) and more biologically determined factors (such as need for risky, stimulating activities or callous personality traits).

3. The connection between economic deprivation and violence is fairly strong but not simple. There is no consensus on exactly how these social factors influence violent behavior.

B1. Family and marital conflict

Family conflict has emerged in research as a very important risk factor in the development of violence in children and youth (104). This conflict may include marital discord (frequent arguments, open disagreements, hostility), family violence (physical aggression against any family member by another member), as well as conflict between parents and children. It is thought that the repeated exposure to verbal or physical conflict in the home increases the likelihood that boys in particular will also use confrontational and violent means to achieve their ends. A common source of conflict between adults is disagreement over parenting practices. Couples usually don't agree on everything about parenting, but handling these conflicts outside of the children's presence and without overt hostility is much healthier for the children.

Implications:

1. Severe and/or persistent marital conflict or violence is a very serious risk factor for children and families. The current and future damage that happens could have long lasting effects on both the children and adult (particularly female) partners.

2. Couples themselves may need couple counseling, empathy and conflict resolution skills to successfully sort out their issues and deal with differences in a productive fashion.

3. Family violence in particular is dangerous both physically and emotionally. Seeking help, support, relief or alternative arrangements may all be necessary to protect vulnerable adults and children.

Limitations:

1. The effect of family and marital conflict on the development of aggression in girls has not been as studied as that on boys. However it is likely that some detrimental effects on girls take place in such an atmosphere.

2. Some of this research is based on reports from children and families themselves. Thus whether people tend to minimize or conceal the degree of conflict needs to be considered.

3. Conflict is not necessarily bad. As will be mentioned under D6 ("conflict resolution"), some conflict is unavoidable; teaching children positive skills with which to cope with differences of opinion can be highly instructive and valuable.

B2. Child abuse and neglect

The relationship between child maltreatment and later violence has been the subject of an increasing amount of research. One such study looked at adults arrested for violent offenses and who had a history of abuse or neglect according to official records (105). These individuals were compared to those without a prior history of abuse. Adults who were sexually abused as children were somewhat less likely to commit a violent offense; those physically abused were more likely to be arrested for a violent act; and those who had been neglected as children were the most likely to commit a violent crime in later life. Other studies have found that the as the frequency and seriousness of the maltreatment increases, the risk for violence also increases. Hence child neglect, even more than other forms of abuse, contributes to the risk of violence in an individual.

Implications:

1. Neglect in particular may be the form of child maltreatment that is most predictive of propensity for later violence. Thus while both physical and sexual abuse are important, more attention, resources, and intervention devoted to neglected children may pay off by decreasing the risk and frequency of future criminal violent offenses.

2. It is not clear what the true extent of neglect is in our society as it is quite likely that more cases are hidden than discovered. Hence adults can practice true prevention themselves by delaying the decision to

have children until they have the internal and external resources necessary to carry out the important tasks of attentive parenting.

3. We don't know exactly why abuse and neglect are associated with increased risk of violence. Possible mechanisms include increase in stress hormones and neurotransmitters in the brain that predispose to aggression. Another possibility is gradual desensitization and loss of emotional feeling and empathy due to abuse, victimization and neglect.

Limitations:

1. To truly examine the association between neglect and violence, one would have to study children from the outset who had versus had not been mistreated and follow them for decades to compare those who were violent to those who were not.

2. Some research finds that physical child abuse increases the risk for general delinquent behavior as opposed to violence specifically. Hence there is some controversy.

3. How studies measure and define maltreatment, neglect, as well as violence in general leads to some concern about different researchers using different definitions, which can influence the results and their interpretation.

B3. *Child rejection*

It has been found that when fathers or mothers openly reject their child, there is an increased risk of antisocial behavior (106). For example, negatively labeling children as being "bad" or "criminal" etc. has been demonstrated to be a risk factor in increasing the child's potential delinquent behavior (107). If children are rejected from home, it is also quite conceivable they could be rejected by other adults and peers due to their behavior. Then the child could essentially become an outcast—someone who only fits in with other delinquent, streetwise and/or substance abusing youth. Children do need to feel they belong and are valued, nurtured and respected; otherwise they will find someplace else where they are, even if this means an antisocial context, rejecting societal norms and values.

Implications:

1. Many families courageously continue to accept and support their youth, despite many difficult experiences with the police, juvenile justice, social service agencies etc. It is possible that some youth who cease their antisocial activities as they grow will value this nurturing and come back or at least keep contact with their families.

2. Before one is on the verge of negatively labeling or physically rejecting youth, every attempt should be made to seek help within the mental health or juvenile justice systems, even though it can be difficult to intervene.

3. Children's behavior may be bad, but hopefully the behavior can be separated from overall feelings about them as people.

Limitations:

1. It takes a great deal of patience and fortitude to continue to patiently accept and support youth who may be violate rules, fail in school, use drugs, or don't help themselves.

2. Even if one attempts to get assistance with a youth's behavior before rejection occurs, it is both difficult to decrease antisocial behaviors with treatment, as well as access treatment itself. The earlier one tries the better.

3. Negatively labeling or rejecting children once probably won't create lasting damage by itself. It is more likely that the repeated conflictual and hostile interactions in families undermine their relationships.

C1. Parental criminality

A number of studies have found that parental criminality is associated with a higher risk of delinquency and aggressiveness in children (108,109). Parental criminality is defined as participating in illegal behaviors that lead to being involved with law enforcement officials. Fathers in particular who have been convicted of theft or assault were in one study much more likely to have sons who participated in those illegal activities than fathers not involved in criminal acts. A British study found that boys with a parent convicted before the child was age 10 were more likely to later be convicted of a violent crime (5). Some of the link may be due to modeling of the illegal and aggressive behavior; perhaps parental support of antisocial and aggressive beliefs systems (e.g. approving of and sanctioning violent behavior) also plays a role. Whether there are genetic factors involved is an area of active research.

Implications:

1. Being a parent or being involved with a parent who has a violent or criminal background may increase the risk that any resulting children will be aggressive or antisocial.

2. One needs careful consideration as to whether having children in such a context is realistically a good idea. The resulting strain on the relationship and increased risk of behavior problems may outweigh possible benefits of having children in this context.

3. If there is a known criminal history in a parent, then early prevention efforts (family support, early parent counseling for behavior problems and building healthy parent-child relations) should be considered.

Limitations:

1. Not every study has substantiated the link between parental criminal history and violence in children. Some have simply found a link between fathers' criminality and sons' property crimes, not personal or violent crimes.

2. It is not clear what mediates the link between parent criminal history and children's violence. Parenting practices, antisocial beliefs and acts, learning or genetic influences may all play a role.

3. The influence of other variables, such as sociological (economic deprivation) and situational factors (provocation, drug use) may sometimes be difficult to interpret when the association between one factor (parental criminality) and one outcome (violence in a child) is examined.

C2. Parental separation from children

There is some evidence that disruption of the parent-child relationship early on may increase the risk of violence in that child. More than one study has found that when couples experience separation or divorce, particularly before the child is 10, the risk of criminal convictions for violence up to early adulthood increases in that child (5). This is true whether one looks at reports by youth themselves or official criminal records. In one study involving a high-risk urban area, leaving home before the age of 16 was linked to increased levels of violent behavior in both men and women as adults (110). It should be noted however, that there is a big difference between a statistical increase in risk as found in studies, and attributing a possible cause of violence to single-parent families, separation, divorce, or leaving home early.

Implications:

1. Family breakdown has been linked to increased risk of violence in the children involved. However, it is not clear if those children would have been more prone to violence in the first place due to several factors, including exposure to marital conflict prior to separation.

2. Parents should try to maintain contact with children post-separation. However, there are circumstances (antisocial behavior, abuse etc.) where this may not be in the child's best interest.

3. These findings don't imply that conflicting partners should necessarily stay together to protect their child against development of behavior problems. While this is important, the child may be better off if he or she is not exposed to serious or frequent conflict or aggression.

Limitations:

1. Divorced or single parents get a lot of grief from our society. We have no way of knowing whether the child would have been better off had the partners stayed together and worked things out, or even if this was possible in the first place.

2. Other influences are surely missing from this equation. The role of peers, education, substances, monitoring etc., especially as the child grows older may surely modifies the effects of previous separation.

3. Leaving home when the family or neighborhood is high-risk may in fact be protective if opportunities open up that steer youth away from risk factors.

C3. Antisocial/Delinquent Siblings

We have previously discussed the influence of parental criminality on child violence. It has also been found that having one or more delinquent siblings by the age of 10 is associated with an increased risk of later convictions for violent offenses. It would appear that this influence increases during childhood and is especially important during the adolescent years. 26% of boys with delinquent siblings were found in a British study to be later convicted of violence compared to 10% of those without delinquent sibs (5). It should be noted that in a Seattle study, the association between delinquent siblings and violence appeared stronger for girls than boys (111). Again it is not clear what these findings mean. There could be inherited factors that predispose children to aggression; growing up under similar influences, models, peers etc. may also play a role.

Implications:

1. Once one child gets into behavioral or legal trouble, the other siblings may be also at risk due to shared or similar risk factors.

2. Girls may be more predisposed than boys to have aggressive or delinquent problems if they have a delinquent sibling.

3. The combination of sibling and delinquent peer influences in adolescence likely greatly increases the risk of antisocial behavior in children who are susceptible.

Limitations:

1. Most of the children (74% in the study above) who have delinquent siblings don't necessarily acquire convictions for violence. Hence, other things must be operating to increase the risk in the vulnerable 26%.

2. It may seem like common sense that having one delinquent sibling increases the risk for having another. However, children in the family can be quite different in their temperaments, personalities, educational achievements and peer influences. Hence again other factors must come into play.

3. It is interesting that in one study girls were found to be more at risk of violence than boys are, if a delinquent sibling was present. How this reconciles with findings of boys being at higher risk of violence in the presence of delinquent peers and gangs is unclear.

C4. Parental mental health

The effects on children of a history of legal involvement and criminal charges in a parent has already been discussed. However, many parents today are stressed and overwhelmed by various expectations and demands. These may include work (sometimes juggling several jobs), financial problems, behavioral problems in their children, housing uncertainties, conflicts with partners, family, or friends, social isolation, and difficulties in either accessing or dealing with community agencies and supports. Such parents are often depressed, burnt out, frustrated and/or angry (112). Having a mental health assessment in such a parent could help by identifying previously undiagnosed depression (for example), leading to medical and/or psychological intervention. Many parents who are treated for depression will describe improved mood, control of their emotions, and expression of positive statements and warmth towards their children.

Implications:

1. Many studies suggest that depression and related problems (coping, substance use, anxiety) are likely under-recognized and treated in our individualistic and "tough it out" society.

2. Improved family functioning could result if the mental effects of chronic stress are identified and worked on.

3. If important risk factors for children include family conflict, neglect, and poor parenting, it is very possible that supporting the parent,

and treating any underlying difficulties may lessen children's risk and protect them from development of future violence.

Limitations:

1. Because of the still pervasive stigma of mental illness, many people chose to ignore, minimize or even worse condemn symptoms of depression or other mental symptoms as signs of weakness.

2. Because of this, many do not seek help when they really need it. Many parents operate on a day to day basis just fighting (sometimes literally) to get through the day's hardships when there may be help available.

3. Medications and counseling won't solve everything but may help people cope better and more realistically with their situations.

C5. Alcoholism

Researchers have attempted to classify types of alcoholism. One relevant type has been designated as Type II alcoholism. This type appears to have some genetic influence (possibly through a dopamine-related gene), and is passed on likely from fathers to sons. Further characteristics of people with this type of alcohol abuse include onset of the alcohol problem before age 25, impulsiveness, a high need for sensation, thrill seeking or risk taking, as well as a history of aggression and violence (113). People with these characteristics are very prone to having antisocial personalities, which means that they violate social norms, can be deceitful, impulsive, aggressive, reckless, irresponsible and/or lack guilt or remorse when they do violate others or societal rules.

Implications:

1. Treatment of the alcohol problem tends to be more complicated in such people due to their personality traits and underlying biological

predisposition to alcohol abuse and violence. The whole issue of whether antisocial personality is treatable will need much more effort and research to answer.

2. Being involved or associating with people who fit this profile can be quite hazardous to one's health! Unfortunately, people with antisocial personalities are very good at hiding their shortcomings as well as conning or manipulating others.

3. Sons of fathers with the above characteristics are more prone to becoming alcoholic and violent. Hence vigilance, early identification and treatment may help change the path so the pattern doesn't repeat.

Limitations:

1. Genetics does not imply destiny. The predisposition to Type II alcoholism does not necessarily imply that everyone so predisposed has to turn out this way. However, effective steps and interventions are still far from clear.

2. Definitions are still being worked on. For example, some researchers feel that the alcoholism in this case may represent just another secondary manifestation of the underlying primary antisocial personality.

3. We need much more genetic and other research to understand the relationship between thrill-seeking, antisocial personality, alcohol abuse, substance abuse, Attention Deficit/Hyperactivity Disorder, and violence.

C6. Parental substance abuse

We have discussed some parental influences such as criminal behavior, alcohol abuse, neglect and mental illness on violence risk. However, what about other non-alcoholic substances? Surprisingly there is little research on substance abuse (other than alcohol) in families and its possible effects on increasing risk of violence or antisocial behavior in children and youth. This may be because some of the research has already captured it (without specifying so) by identifying parental antisocial behavior as a risk factor, given many people with antisocial personalities abuse substances. Further, many who drink to excess also use other substances and this can be hard to factor out. Likely any study would have to distinguish between hard substances (cocaine, heroin) and softer ones, such as marijuana. It is regrettable that we do not know more about the role of substances in the families and environments in which these aggressive youth reside.

Implications:

1. Common substances that increase violence risk in adults include cocaine, amphetamines, and PCP, also known as phencyclidine (114). Youth who have access to such substances or are exposed to use by family members and others may be more prone to use them. However, research in this area is lacking.

2. Commonly, substance abuse interacts with other things such as the user's personality, predisposition to violence, any existing mental illness, and contextual factors such as poverty or stress. Thus any contribution towards violence would have to take these other factors into account.

3. Opioids (e.g. heroin), marijuana, and benzodiazepines (e.g. valium) are much less commonly associated with violence.

Limitations:

1. The lack of research done in the area of association between family substance abuse and children's risk of violence does not mean such an association does or does not exist.

2. Much of the existing research into the effects of some substances (e.g. anabolic steroids) has been retrospective (relying on memory or historical documentation), has not always been systematic, has not compared users to control groups who don't use, and lacks information about use of other drugs.

3. It is unclear what increases the risk of antisocial behavior over the long term. Possibilities include: the acute intoxicating effects of the drugs, the effects of chronic use, and the effects of social factors (associating with others who use, some of whom may be more antisocial).

D1. Curfews

Curfews can be set either at the level of a family or an entire community. The afternoon hours of 2:00 p.m. until 6:00 p.m. tend to account for a large number of juvenile offenses. However, most violent crimes involving youth, such as robbery, rape, homicide and serious assault, tend to occur between 10:00 p.m. and 1:00 a.m. Trying to keep these youth out of trouble through a curfew is thought to be one possible approach of many to address this issue (115). If youth are accountable for their hours and actions and their whereabouts are known, it is possible that the crime rate could drop at these peak hours. This has been identified as a promising approach at the community level. Those communities who have enacted curfews for adolescents report reductions in crime from between 10% and 27%.

Implications:

1. Having youth report in or come home at a certain time may have some effect in reducing their potential to engage in serious or violent crime during peak hours.

2. Parents need support from law enforcement and communities to effectively set and monitor curfews. It would be difficult to set, monitor, and enforce such a standard by oneself in isolation.

3. Communities and neighborhoods, especially in high crime areas, may wish to consider enacting curfews as a way to decrease the potential for crime.

Limitations:

1. It is not yet really clear if curfews are worth the social cost of police and community involvement. It may sound good in theory, but takes considerable coordination and support for authorities to make it happen successfully.

2. Parents by themselves have very little leverage to enforce curfews and consequence their violations. It is likely that the very youth who rebel against rules and authority are the ones that need this family and community response.

3. If contemplated, the public needs to be informed and behind this move so it will not be perceived as another policy of over-regulation. A public/police partnership can much further enhance of crime prevention.

D2. Commitment to social/institutional values

While controversial, it would appear that individuals and families who develop commitment to actions valued by social institutions have a lower risk of violent behavior (116). Essentially, this means that incorporating the values espoused by progressive schools, religious organizations, or socially committed families can be protective. Thus, positive attitudes towards school achievement and education, positive social values articulated and demonstrated by prosocial religious groups (regardless of denomination), and positive attitudes towards family and family life can mitigate other risk factors. The key ingredient that links these groups is likely that a philosophy of social connection, treating others with respect, and helping others, amongst other related values can likely help mitigate the risk of violence in otherwise vulnerable children or youth.

Implications:

1. Children's attitudes to family, people, school, and community are fostered early and developed throughout childhood. Reinforcement of the positive attitudes embodied by such groups can foster children's healthy emotional development.

2. Instilling in children and youth a sense of community and school responsibility from early on can help ward off later antisocial influences.

3. While fewer people may be involved in organized religion than decades ago, there is some evidence that being affiliated with some such group reduces the risk of violence in involved persons.

Limitations:

1. The nature of the exact ingredients that help protect people against violence is controversial. This is particularly true when it comes to involvement with organizations such as schools or religious groups.

2. Instilling prosocial and pro-educational values is easier said than done. Many people become disenfranchised, often with good reason, from society's institutions.

3. People are more wary today of authority, institutions, religion etc. Thus such values and affiliations do take time to nurture and to take effect, like any positive trusting relationship.

D3. Social support

Having social supports outside the family has consistently been found to be a protective factor against development of violence. Social support can be in the form of extended family support (grandparents, aunts, uncles, cousins etc.), supportive friends, community involvement (mental health support, drop-in centers, parenting centers, religious affiliation etc.) or other societal involvement (athletics, clubs etc.). One very relevant research finding is that in families with many risk factors, including social isolation, sparse networks, and weak social support, child abuse was more likely than in families with stronger social involvement (117). Hence from a violence prevention viewpoint, the more one can engage others outside the immediate family structure, the more protected the child is from becoming antisocial.

Implications:

1. Community agencies are there to try to help decrease isolation and increase resources for families. Prudent use of such external networks can help families deal with the stresses of life, loneliness, and parenting.

2. Parents and adults need relief to re-energize themselves to effectively deal with the children in their care and charge. Hence having at least one outlet in the community, whether it is a social support or hobby, can be a worthy break from the stress and routine.

3. Children who see their parents and other important adults in their lives engaged in community supports and activities may grow up to have emotionally healthy and prosocial attitudes towards adults, and society in general. Isolation and disengagement from society characterizes many antisocial and violent youth.

Limitations:

1. It can be threatening to some adults to try to engage a community agency or other such institution. Past experience, mistrust, and disenchantment can make it difficult to reach out for support.

2. Time is also a limiting factor. With chronic stress from many avenues, some adults and families are simply run off their feet. However, setting goals and important priorities, such as social contact with the outside world can be effective from both modeling (for the child) and violence prevention perspectives.

3. The various systems (government, agencies, education, legal, mental health etc.) outside stressed families can do more to reach out to marginalized and isolated families, who often carry the highest risk of violence in their children. Societies can help their citizens feel more supported to decrease alienation in families and youth.

D4. Modeling decision-making

Decision-making is a core skill that is part of many violence prevention programs for children and adolescents (118). The idea is that children often make impulsive interpretations and decisions that can lead to aggressive or adverse consequences. They often haven't developed the foresight to think through the consequences of a number of possible alternative decisions before taking action. As parents and adults, we can greatly help children by demonstrating out loud the following: some of the decisions we face, the information we have to consider before making a decision, the alternative possibilities and pathways, the risks and benefits of different courses of action, and anticipated consequences of the decision(s). This sounds complicated but can be done fairly simply for children to learn and ask questions about different choices they and adults face in life. They can then apply this to their own life choices and situations.

Implications:

1. Children should be exposed to simple decisions at first. "What to make for dinner" could be one of many examples in which one has to balance ease of preparation, time, people's preferences, clean up etc. and come to a somewhat efficient conclusion.

2. Even small children should be encouraged to ask questions about how adults made decisions—job choices, selection of home, schools etc. They will learn over time to appreciate greater complexity as time goes on.

3. Effective decisions are a combination of facts and feelings. Sometimes it's better to go with one's head than heart and vice versa, but one never knows this ahead of time. Children can be taught to learn from decisions that did not have the intended outcome rather than pine away in defeat.

Limitations:

1. As with most instructional activities, talking aloud about one's decisions takes more time than simply deciding in your head. However, over the long term, children's exposure to some of this decision-making process should help them develop the skills to make informed choices.

2. Making effective decisions is only one of many problem-solving skills that can help protect children from aggressive decisions and actions. Others will be discussed shortly.

3. Sometimes, one can thoroughly think out a problem and still have a bad outcome (for example, buying a new car or appliance that turns out to be a lemon).

D5. Modeling negotiation

Another common social skill is negotiating with others (119). Adults can teach children a great deal, as children observe how adults conduct business both within and outside of the home. Being polite to others, listening attentively, being articulate and assertive with one's opinion, finding a common area of agreement during a discussion or conflict, and compromising to achieve a common resolution are all necessary skills in life. People like to be treated with respect in any dialogue and children quickly pick up when one side is being angry, unreasonable, demanding, or vengeful; they will then learn that this is how to negotiate with others. There are many parts to successful negotiation, although certainly listening and thinking are key to the others.

Implications:
1. Children absorb much more non-verbal and verbal information for which we adults don't give them credit. Thus careful modeling of negotiation in front of children would be desirable.
2. Negotiation, like decision-making, is a skill that takes some practice. There will be both easy and difficult negotiations in life. Children gently but firmly need to understand that they cannot always get what they want.
3. Children will have many opportunities to practice negotiation— with siblings, parents, school children, friends, or extra curricular activities. Encouraging them to both talk about and continue their struggles will reinforce their efforts.

Limitations:
1. Negotiating is harder than simply being demanding. However, negotiation skills should help children get through life's struggles,

effectively talk to people, and get at least some, if not most of what they want or need.

2. Despite effective negotiation skills, some times people just aren't successful if the person or institution they are dealing with has much more power and less interest in serving them. Children and adults sometimes need to persist but other times simply move on.

3. Various books and viewpoint have been written about effective negotiation. No one way works all the time.

D6. Conflict resolution

Children quickly learn that their world is full of conflict. How they handle conflict often helps determine how many friends they have, who their friends are, their reputation, their opportunities, their potential isolation, and positive as well as negative consequences for their actions. Modeling conflict resolution skills is similar to negotiation, except that negotiation doesn't always involve conflict. How adults handle conflict with each other, whether in front of the child or behind closed doors is quite instructional for the youngster's view of how people deal with each other "in the heat of the moment". While anger is natural during conflict, there are many skills to be modeled. These include again listening to the other's argument, reflecting back to them what was said, empathy for their position or situation, managing one's own anger or emotions, learning when to take a break, compromising or staying the course, and of course resolution and implementation.

Implications:

1. Successful conflict resolution is more about keeping one's head and cool than losing it and achieving nothing. Handling heated

emotions is difficult, but anger management and resolving conflicts are a major skill often missing in violent children (120).

2. Children are often exposed to marital conflict. They could learn from the verbal and non-verbal communication how to deal with conflict in relationships and still carry on in a caring fashion. If tempers flare, it is better that children not be exposed to repeated angry or aggressive outbursts from parents.

3. Much of conflict resolution is having the other person be heard, empathized with and validated. Teaching children these skills alone can be helpful in their dealings with others.

Limitations:

1. Like negotiation, conflict resolution skills build over time with practice and confidence. Driving a car becomes more comfortable and automatic a year after obtaining one's license than during the driving test.

2. Not all conflicts can be resolved due to stubbornness, aggression, or miscommunication. What is important is increasing one's odds of success by repeatedly using the skills discussed. No strategy is always successful despite many expert books on the subject. The important theme is to demonstrate non-aggressive ways to deal with others and resolve impasses.

D7. Empathy

Empathy is essentially the verbal and emotional expression of one's acknowledgement and appreciation of another's feelings or struggles. It is thought that empathy and aggression are not compatible with each other and thus training children to be empathic may decrease the potential for violence (121). Empathy training and modeling can start in the home, starting with the relationship between each parent and child. It is important that children, who tend to be somewhat self-centered anyway, have adults recognize their feelings and struggles. A child who in turn becomes more empathic with others will have stronger friendships, popularity, openness with others, growth, and ability to deal with conflicts. A small percentage of children are growing up with callous or unemotional personality traits. It is important to show these children early on that being empathic is actually in their best interest and can further their own goals.

Implications:

1. The group of children who very early on (in preschool) exhibit callousness towards others may be a group that later is responsible for much crime and violence. Thus early work on building their empathy skills with emphasis on the benefits to them may be preventive.

2. Empathy training is becoming increasingly used in schools to increase conflict resolution, decrease violence, and regain a culture of cooperation and socialization.

3. Empathy, negotiation, conflict resolution, and effective decision-making are all related. Thus working on them singly or together can give your child effective skills with which to grow and develop.

Limitations:

1. Adults who are stressed, isolated or unsupported can be themselves exhibit poor empathy. Thus they may need to acknowledge this and work on their own skills before or while teaching their children.

2. Empathy training is not easy. People's natural inclination to be self-interested often gets in the way. But the gains by being more empathic, altruistic and cooperative usually outweigh the risks.

3. There is debate about whether empathy can even be taught. Some people are just naturally more emotionally attuned to others. However the cost of not trying may be too high to ignore.

D8. Universal values

Universal values are those values or beliefs that are common to prosocial and law-abiding citizens and societies. They are much less controversial than other values-based systems. Universal values include things such as honesty, discipline, tolerance of others, respect for others, integrity, reliability, a strong work ethic, caring and kindness towards others. Some school boards have introduced these in their curricula (122). However such traits and development of character can also be taught in the home and elsewhere. These values are not connected with any particular religious group but represent what characteristics a person should have to function well and be well regarded in any society. It is probably best that such universal values education be stressed, taught and reinforced in several settings for children to develop good character.

Implications:
1. A good education, both in the home and in school, should likely include some discussion about common moral values that our society should espouse in its children, youth and adults.

2. For children to actually believe and internalize these values, they will likely need to observe the adults around them in various settings exhibit these qualities. Actions speak louder than mere words.

3. Every experience and interaction a child will have likely presents some opportunity to discuss a universal value. For example, rewarding children for their use of honesty or kindness is a great way to reinforce its expression until these virtues become part of their characters.

Limitations:

1. Not everyone can consistently act in a way that demonstrates universal values. Thus adults need to be open with children when they err or when a situation demands self interest (e.g. abuse or bullying).

2. Circumstances sometimes make instilling universal values difficult. Time, stress, equating universal values with certain religious philosophies can lessen general interest in conversing about good moral values.

3. Short term interventions or courses tend to have less effect on school and home climates. Better results are likely when values education, along with other violence prevention programs, is deeply embedded in the everyday school and staff interactions and culture.

D9. Family therapy

Families who have many risk factors usually have difficulty in changing or reducing these risk factors by themselves. Thus research has indicated that certain specific types of family therapy that focus on behaviors and family processes (e.g. conflict in the family) may be more successful at helping families than others (123). In particular, those therapies that focus on increasing parenting skills and practices (such as predictability, monitoring, positive reinforcement), decreasing harsh or coercive patterns (abuse, verbal hostility), and improving family relations (closeness, clarity, communications, cohesion) tend to do better. Better means reducing children's later risk and commitment of violent offenses and drug use. Such therapies, notably Functional Family Therapy and Multisystemic Therapy, are intense for families and therapists but have been shown to reduce the risk of future violence in adolescents.

Implications:

1. One of the most important determinants of success is actually sticking with the therapy. Families who drop out obviously don't do as well as those who complete a course of therapy.

2. Although adolescents tend to be harder to change than children, such behavioral family therapies have been shown to reduce disruptive behavior in affected youth. This is accomplished by improving the family's functioning and their connection to the surrounding community.

3. Children and youth who are already violent can be helped, at least to some degree by such focussed and behaviorally oriented therapies.

Limitations:

1. While these therapies do help when the groups of families are statistically analyzed, it is not at all clear how to help those families who discontinue treatment or are not improved after intervention.

2. Success in many studies is measured by youth staying out of the prison system longer or having lower offending rates than non-treated youth and families. Thus achieving dramatic change is much less realistic than lessening the risk of further criminal behavior.

3. These therapies are unfortunately not yet widely available or disseminated. Hence many agencies and systems are making do with available resources and having some difficulty in engaging and helping these youth and families.

CHAPTER FOUR: FACTORS WITHIN THE COMMUNITY

Community Risk Factors
Community Protective Factors

A1. Neighborhood Disorganization

Neighborhood or community disorganization has been assessed and measured by looking at adolescents' perceptions of the levels of crime, selling of drugs, presence of gangs, and availability of housing support in their communities (124). Not surprisingly, it has been found that a lower level of organization, embodied by higher neighborhood criminal activity and poor housing was associated with a higher level of violent acts by youth in that neighborhood. Living in such a neighborhood often makes escaping violence or drugs extremely difficult due to the surrounding environment. Many people in such neighborhoods often live in continuous fear and vigilance due to the harsh conditions. Youth who grew up in these disorganized settings tended to involve themselves in a greater variety of violent acts by age 18 than those who lived elsewhere.

Implications:

1. While the individual is ultimately responsible for his or her own actions, we are also products of our environments, whether enriched or adverse. The contribution of such environments is often underemphasized in our culture of blame.

2. Making neighborhoods more cohesive with a sense of community and safety should be a higher priority for all citizens and levels of government.

3. It is extremely difficult to raise children safely without fear of negative influence or violence in such neighborhoods. Thus such families, whether single parent or not, need more support under these difficult circumstances.

Limitations:

1. While these sociological findings have been known for decades, it is not clear how much is actually being done to address these underlying issues.

2. Not all violence is the result of poorly organized neighborhoods, as the Columbine shooting tragedy taught us. Thus again, no one factor explains everything.

3. Many bright and upstanding citizens have their humble roots in difficult neighborhoods. Hence very resilient children will somehow thrive and rise above their circumstances.

A2. Poor neighborhood attachment

The attachment that children have for their neighborhoods has also been studied (18). This is related to neighborhood organization. It basically involves children's perceptions of safety within their neighborhood and affection for their neighborhood. In one study pre-adolescent children were assessed again as teenagers four to six years later. Essentially, the degree of attachment to one's neighborhood was most useful by age 16. That is the less attached a youth was by age 16, the more likely he or she would have been involved in serious crime. However, this association was relatively less important than that found for the degree of neighborhood disorganization. Children and youth who feel less safe and secure in their neighborhoods may be more prone to paranoid-like thinking (being continuously vigilant to signs of danger) and thus be reactively more aggressive.

Implications:

1. Children who continuously feel unsafe may be susceptible to aggressive thinking. The idea that potential enemies, threats and danger could be lurking imminently, leads one to see danger everywhere. Hence these children are more reactive, more prone to aggressive reactions, and look for signs of potential aggression, even in neutral circumstances.

2. Youth in particular need more ways to reconnect with their communities. In times of economic prosperity when jobs are plentiful, this happens naturally as youth often work and live in their communities. However, in desperate times youth can be much more disconnected.

3. Disconnection and detachment from one's neighborhood could theoretically be a good thing if one is looking for positive opportunities outside of a disorganized and unsafe community.

Limitations:

1. Some of the studies used reports from study subjects themselves to generate the data. Objective measures of safety and attachment would be more reliable, although difficult in practice.

2. The degree of neighborhood prosperity, drug selling, and crime were much more predictive of the degree of violence than attachment to the community.

3. We don't know if degree of attachment to one's neighborhood is necessarily better in "better neighborhoods". Thus comparing adolescent attachment to a disorganized neighborhood versus a more organized one would be useful.

A3. Exposure to neighborhood violence

High levels of exposure to violence have been found in many surveys. In a survey of fifth and sixth graders in Washington DC, 43% had witnessed a mugging, 31% had witnessed a shooting, 22% had been victimized in a mugging, and 11% had been victims of a shooting (126). Equally startling, a 1995 survey of 3700 high school students in Denver, Colorado and Cleveland, Ohio found that half of the boys and over one-third of the girls had witnessed a shooting in the previous year, and over one-quarter of the boys reported having been shot at within the past year (127). Chronic exposure to serious and frequent violence has been shown by research to be lead to vulnerability to many psychological symptoms. These include those of post-traumatic stress disorder, somewhat similar to soldiers, victims of war, earthquakes or other severe trauma.

Implications:

1. Psychological symptoms should be looked for in children from high-risk neighborhoods. These symptoms include aggression, anxiety, depression, concentration problems, heightened vigilance, emotional reactivity, substance abuse, nightmares, and emotional detachment.

2. Victims of violence exposure likely need at least basic needs met (safety, security, emotional warmth, routine), as well as processing about the meaning of their experiences, with provision of hope for the future.

3. Children's mental health agencies ideally need to provide more services for victims of violence or exposure. Most services are geared currently towards those who actually are violent.

Limitations:

1. According to one study, about two-thirds of children did not experience psychological trauma from exposure to violence. What distinguishes these children from the other one-third needs more study.

2. Most children and adults who have more overt behavior (e.g. violence) tend to have better access to programs than do victims. Further, the mental health system likely would have difficulty absorbing the potentially large numbers of victims who suffer psychological distress.

3. Whether such identification, counseling, and support would assist when disorganized neighborhoods persist in perpetuating such symptoms is as yet unclear.

B1. After school recreation programs

As previously mentioned, after school is a high-risk time for youth. Recreation programs typically attempt to occupy their time, provide some structure for leisure and play, as well as promote prosocial values and a sense of attachment and belonging. Some sociologists and others have suggested that schools themselves are underutilized after classes end for the day. They could be organized to provide remedial academic help, mentoring, as well as arts, crafts, sports, music, theatre, hobbies and computer classes (126). For example, a 32-month program in Ottawa, Canada in a low-income housing area provided sports, music, dance, and other activities. During the duration of the study there was a 75% reduction in the number of juveniles arrested in the area, compared to before the project, providing some evidence of effect (127).

Implications:

1. Boys and Girls clubs are an excellent example of programs that can engage children and youth, particularly those from high-risk backgrounds.

2. There are perhaps many adults in the community, particularly retired folks, who might enjoy being involved in supervising or sharing their talents and experience with youth in organized after school programs.

3. Youth can be engaged in such programs, particularly if multiple activities and interests that appeal to many are provided.

Limitations:

1. Cost has typically been cited as a deterrent to more widespread use of schools or other facilities after class. However, this must be measured against the social and economic cost of crime.

2. Sustaining such programs is necessary because the Ottawa study quoted above also showed that 16 months after the program ended, the difference had narrowed considerably between the group of youth that had received the recreational program and the one that did not.

3. It would take considerable coordination and organization to get and retain youth in these programs, as well as hire people and/or obtain volunteers for their successful maintenance.

B2. Possible community prevention strategies

There are few studies devoted to what works at the community level in terms of violence prevention. However, researchers have presented several possible ideas (128). Focussing primarily on the continuous threat of violence in some areas may be perpetuating people's suspiciousness in vulnerable communities. Hence, recommendations have included increasing profiles for public events and displays of peaceful community activities. In Chicago, for example, awards are given to those who help make a neighborhood more peaceful. Decreasing isolation by such things as business promotions, or community activities such as plays may be some ways to get people out of their homes and interested in nonviolent, peaceful, and prosocial norms for their neighborhoods. Enforcing housing violations and other illegal activities, as well as providing citizens with tools to work with police (e.g. pagers) are other ways to re-engage the public. Rewards for children and youth who behave positively may raise the profile of good behavior. Creativity, leadership, and resources will be necessary for success.

Implications:

1. Effective tools are available to revive broken communities. However, implementation requires coordination between government, business, and citizens so all can benefit and take pride in the accomplishments.

2. The focus on positive public modeling and rewards for good behavior may slowly reduce the exclusive emphasis on fear, threat, violence, deviance, and criminality.

3. Communities in the post-war era were much different. People were outdoors more, looked out for each other, were friendlier to each other, worked hard and felt they had goals and aspirations. Hopefully with some of the steps above, and many other innovative strategies across the continent, citizens can reclaim their communities.

Limitations:

1. Any community project should likely be carefully implemented with broad stakeholder input and evaluation to really demonstrate improvement.

2. "Communities That Care" is an extremely comprehensive program in many American cities. It is very likely that such well-organized

and holistic approaches that use a risk and protective factor model will be more successful, but will take much more coordination.

3. The notion of quick fixes has been largely disproven by research. For violence prevention to work at any level (family, school, or community), requires time, resources, commitment, and comprehensiveness of strategies. These will likely prove to be more effective and durable than looking for "the solution".

CHAPTER FIVE: FACTORS WITHIN SOCIETY

Societal Risk Factors
Society Protective Factors

A1. Extreme deprivation

Numerous studies have documented that economic inequality and poverty have been major contributors toward societal violence over the past 100 years. These findings have been robust whether in different regions, cities, or countries. In the United States of course, the variable of race is also very salient to these social issues, as social and economic inequality often occur together. However, it is becoming more clear that the very poorest communities, especially those where disadvantaged visible minorities reside, tend to have the highest levels of violence. For example, one study looked at Columbus, Ohio and found that higher poverty levels were linked to higher violence levels; further, the poorest neighborhoods (in which over 40% live below the poverty level), suffered from extremely high levels of violence (129). Hence there is a qualitative difference even between various levels of poverty in terms of the correlation with the prevalence of violence.

Implications:

1. The extreme deprivation could account for the association between violence and race. Whether there are other factors that contribute to the high homicide rate for young African-Americans has been hotly debated.

2. As discussed previously, nations that are more generous and socially conscious tend to have lower overall homicide rates. While this has

not been the philosophy in place in the United States generally, perhaps it is time for a change.

3. The so-called "economic boom" has not been one for everyone. Many if not most would agree that the recent good times have been of more benefit to those above the poverty line than those beneath.

Limitations:

1. Greater coordination between the criminological, sociologic, and mental health researchers would greatly enhance our understanding of the causes and correlates of violence in society.

2. Further exploration is required as to what is the nature of the increased vulnerability of poor African-American communities to violence—availability of weapons, drugs, cultural erosion, impact of exposure or other factors.

3. While all this research is well and good, it still has not necessarily translated into actual action, therapeutic and supportive policy, and improvement in the quality of lives of our poorest citizens.

A2. Demoralization

It has already been suggested that there are very strong links between economics, inequality and antisocial behavior. But why is this so? Sociologists believe that the missing explanation lies in the meaning that people as well as society as a whole attach to such things as material worth. In North American culture, much if not most emphasis is placed on material wealth. Hence it is argued that this increased pressure ("strain") when insufficient resources or opportunities are available to all leads to illegal or deviant behavior, including violent means to ends. Sub-cultural norms that favor or glorify violence, toughness, conning others, or the drug abuse industry become more the standard when the larger cultural norms of material gain are out of reach. Such a philosophy then may make it less likely that regular job or prosocial opportunities will be attractive and taken when they are available.

Implications:

1. The meaning individuals and societies place on wealth, its quick acquisition, and mainstream opportunities to achieve can help us understand why some youth, gangs and others become so disenfranchised and demoralized with such institutions of education, justice, citizenship, and the workplace (130).

2. The increasing emphasis on materialism in society likely contributed greatly to the decline of social values such as honesty, integrity, altruism and cooperation.

3. There are huge social forces (culture, peers, media etc.) that influence youth in various directions. Likely these must be discussed openly, their interpretations and meanings evaluated, and other social values taught and modeled in order for our society to move forward.

Limitations:

1. It is difficult to go against the herd and trends when everyone is so obsessed with money and advancement. Money is a necessity to survive, but some of us are surviving more than others.

2. Teaching children from an early age the meaning of money in the context of other values (hard work, patience, honesty, cooperation etc.) may be one way to counter the overwhelming drive to material gain and the behaviors that tempt one when that gain is out of reach.

3. Because social forces are so powerful, the cost of living so high, the demoralization of disadvantaged citizens so great, the drive for material accumulation and success so unrelenting, the "strain"

between what people have, what they value, and what society values may get worse before it gets better.

A3. Social disorganization

Social disorganization refers to the erosion and decreasing number of previously stable social and community institutions. It has been well documented that those communities with a stronger presence of such institutions (which can include churches, organizations, extended families, agencies etc.) have relatively less juvenile crime even under difficult economic circumstances than communities with weaker social structures (131). A frequently quoted example is the country of Ireland. It has strong community institutions (especially the church), has been relatively poorer than other European nations, and yet has a low level of youth homicide. Weaker family structures may also play a role in other countries by reducing adolescent attachment and adult supervision. It is when one combines economic deprivation, erosion of societal institutions, family breakdown and demoralization as has happened in many areas of Western civilization, the rates of youth violence tend to be particularly high.

Implications:

1. There are no simple explanations for youth violence. A culmination of individual, family, and societal forces mold people's risk in increasingly understood ways to produce antisocial behavior.

2. Major investment in high-risk communities will be necessary to seriously address the plight of disadvantaged people caught in our current social forces.

3. Early attachment to existing social structures (school, church, agencies, neighborhood events etc.) may help children and youth learn new skills, meet new people, and keep them occupied and supervised.

Limitations:

1. All the data that exists is retrospective (meaning it's essentially historical). One would ultimately have to shift societal forces and values, particularly in urban and other high-risk areas to really test out if change is possible.

2. Planning for economic downturns in terms of having venues for high-risk youth (when work is not available) may be more acceptable to the public, business, and government. It may also be easier than trying to change fairly large and evolving (or devolving as the case may be) social institutions, such as the emphasis on wealth creation, individualism etc.

3. There is little formal research as to what goes wrong in relatively economically advantaged communities who experience violence (such as Columbine). However the same social disintegration of institutions and community norms may affect suburbs and urban areas alike.

A4. Inner cities

Not all poor disadvantaged communities are created equal. There are differences between urban poor ("outer" city) and urban poor inner city neighborhoods. The difference boils down to the relatively greater access and availability of resources as well as slightly higher but still impoverished income of non-inner city communities. Inner city areas generally have very high poverty, higher crime, more single-parent families, more rental accommodation, and more public housing. One study found that aggression and delinquent behavior were respectively 2.5 and 2.8 times the national average in inner-city areas (132). Also, increased risks of school dropout and adolescent pregnancy have been reported in inner cities.

Hence there is added stress and risk of living in inner cities; the effects on individual and family life there are more profound than in any other locale.

Implications:

1. Focussing on strengthening the particularly vulnerable circumstances of inner cities could pay huge dividends in reducing crime and improving quality of life.

2. Poverty alone does not cause crime. When combined with other social forces, particular groups of people or communities would be more at risk.

3. Many people become trapped in dangerous inner city neighborhoods simply because they may be demoralized, other opportunities are not available, and society has difficulty facing and dealing with complex and vulnerable groups. However, children do deserve the same basic resources of food, security, and education regardless of where they live or what their family incomes are.

Limitations:

1. It is easier to avoid than confront the problems facing our inner cities. Thus gated communities are becoming more common, enabling people with more resources to pretend that the problem is elsewhere.

2. The societal trend towards the overarching importance of individual need and economic success over the good for all has likely greatly damaged the social equality and fabric of our society. Because this trend overwhelmingly benefits those in positions of power or authority, there is little motivation for radical change at the present time.

3. Because of this trend towards individuality and the complexity of our deteriorating society, solutions will come from those with clear social consciences that understand the value of society's social capital—its citizens.

A5. *Availability of Weapons*

A survey carried out by the Center for Disease Control indicated that almost 20% of all surveyed students reported carrying a weapon (knife, razor, club, or gun) on at least one occasion in the previous month (133). Of these, 55% carried a knife or razor, 24% a club, and 21% a firearm. One study compared Seattle with Vancouver, which is stricter in its handgun laws. It found that the rate of aggravated assault with a firearm in Seattle was 7.7 times greater than that in Vancouver; also, the risk of being murdered by a handgun was 4.8 times greater in Seattle, despite similar rates of robbery, assault, and homicide by a non-firearm (134). On the other hand, there is some evidence (135) that defending oneself with a gun results in less frequent injury to the victim (17.4%) than other means (knife—40.3%, fighting back—50.8%, running away—34.9%, not resisting—24.7%). Hence the relationship between guns and violence is not a simple one.

Implications:

1. Firearms are likely only one important factor that contributes to youth violence. They may be more a means to an end as many if not most murderers already have a history of violence and may find other ways to carry out their actions.

2. Firearms are an example of a situational variable, as are the use of alcohol, motive of the offender, actions of the victim, the role of bystanders and the relationship between offender and victim. Hence it is difficult to attribute cause to a single entity under many conditions of violence.

3. Handguns can also be used for defense. Thus how a gun is used is important in addition to its availability.

Limitations:

1. Situational factors such as gun use need to be studied more in order to understand the relationship between them, individual factors, and social factors.

2. Situations with similar circumstances (availability of weapons, alcohol use, conflict etc.) where violence did not occur are understudied. Thus understanding the risk of violence is hampered by an inability to compare various situations with similar risks and circumstances.

3. It is unclear if there are real differences between gun owners and those who do not possess a firearm. Also, the actual motivation behind firearm murders (to murder, threaten, or hurt) is not often distinguished in studies.

A6. Gangs

The role and experiences of ethnic groups in North America in gang formation has already been previously discussed under "diversity" (Chapter One, B3). A 1996 survey found that 300 cities in America had collectively 16,000 gangs representing over 500,000 members, 95% of them male (136). More small cities and towns today have gangs than every before. Gang related violence and homicides do appear to be increasing but the reasons are not totally clear. Gangs today have several functions. One is simply economic survival of members by informal work (including the drug trade), using violence as the currency of regulation of their industry. Another factor is expression of masculinity: different gangs and member use joblessness, multiple weapons, drug use or sales, and violence to varying degrees as expressions of their power. Finally, there are increases in prison gangs, some of which continue to operate outside jail.

Implications:

1. Gang and ex-gang members who are trying to improve their lives should be assisted with job training and substance abuse treatment. People who are trying to become functioning citizens of society should be encouraged.

2. Ex-gang members can be effectively incorporated into prevention and intervention efforts regarding youth gangs. Dissuading youth from joining gangs is a difficult but worthy goal.

3. Gangs do provide some attachment, security, identity, social status and economic reward for youth who don't otherwise have these opportunities. Thus youth will need realistic support from families and society to avoid gang incentives.

Limitations:

1. Without viable employment opportunities for economic and personal growth, the gang problem is likely to worsen as time goes on.

2. The shifting values towards increasing materialism, individualism, and violence will be hard to modify unless all levels of government, individuals and corporations model emphasizing responsibility to the community at large.

3. There are diverse pathways to gang membership. Further research is vitally needed to understand the transitions from groups to gangs. Alienated youth do join gangs but so do youth who are aggressive, possess leadership qualities and are well connected in their communities.

A7. Delinquent peers in society

The growth in adolescent violence in the last decade tends to be attributed to the increase in the number of adolescents newly engaging in such behavior, as opposed to an increase in the number of children who continue their violent behaviors in adolescence (2). This distinction is important, as adolescent peers who are delinquent then become an increasingly important societal risk. Violence is thought to spread especially where delinquent peers congregate, whether this be in schools, gangs or in the community. It would appear that adolescents who newly engage in antisocial behavior tend to mimic early-onset chronic offenders, which then of course serves to increase their involvement in more and more delinquent behavior (137). This may partially account for the great difficulty in changing this pathway during adolescence.

Implications:

1. From a prevention standpoint, engaging children prior to adolescence in prosocial peers and activities is worthwhile. This may help by decreasing the association with delinquent peers.

2. Grouping delinquent youth together, whether in or outside treatment has been shown to be quite detrimental; the reinforcement of antisocial attitudes and actions only increases the risk of future antisocial behavior.

3. "Instigators"—older youth with longer criminal histories, are likely responsible for much of the spread of antisocial behavior as they tend to attract less experienced youth. Hence first time offenders have a small window of opportunity for rehabilitation before their behavior escalates.

Limitations:

1. Much if not most of delinquent peer behavior happens where there is no adult supervision. It is impossible to observe and monitor youth 100% of the time.

2. Exactly how delinquent peers increase risk is still being researched. How they influence and are influenced by their own and others' behaviors is still under investigation.

3. If it is true that most of the spread of adolescent violence is due to new antisocial behavior in adolescence and association with delinquent peers, then in theory these youth should decrease their violent ways as they grow into adulthood. It may require some debate as to which group (early versus later onset) requires more attention and services.

A8. Bullying

The public is increasingly aware that bullying of children and youth occurs within and outside of the school system. One example, amongst others, of a successful anti-bullying school program was set up originally in Norway (138). Four components were highlighted. The first involved all school staff in elementary schools receiving a booklet about bullying, victimization, and suggestions for staff about intervention and prevention. Secondly, all families in Norway with school-age children received an information package about bullying with suggestions. Also, a video about the lives of two adolescent teenage bullying victims was available at a low cost. Finally, student surveys were used to plan further interventions. Subsequent evaluation found that twenty months after the program, the prevalence of bullying for each age group had dropped substantially.

Implications:

1. Tackling a school or social problem such as bullying requires a comprehensive educational or community approach with proper evaluation to demonstrate results.

2. Awareness, sensitivity, and intervention about victimization require the involvement of youth, school and home to achieve positive effects. Hence cooperation between school and home is vital.

3. Encouraging children to open up and disclose bullying does require trust that the adults will actually act and do something about it. Otherwise, there is obviously a chance of further victimization and retaliation by bullies. Hence bullying should be taken seriously when disclosed.

Limitations:

1. Because effecting change with regards to bullying requires coordination and cooperation between students, school, and parents, clear leadership is vital, otherwise parties can become discouraged.

2. Evaluation of some bullying programs shows that they can have relatively smaller effects on older children (that is, the programs produced greater reduction in bullying among younger children).

3. Whether the anti-bullying program has alleviated difficulties of individual victims is unclear. For example, in the study quoted above, 13 year olds before the program were compared to 13 year olds after the program, showing a decrease at this age level. However, these obviously would not represent the same children.

A9. Peer rejection

Peer rejection, teasing, and bullying have been implicated in some recent high profile school shootings in the United States. Rejection by peers has consistently been linked with aggression in childhood, later school dropout, criminality, and interpersonal or relationship problems in adulthood. One group that has been documented to be particularly at high risk for rejection consists of those children with both Attention

Deficit Hyperactivity Disorder and aggressive behavior. For example, in one study, children rejected socially by classmates in kindergarten and grade one were noted to be more aggressive and hyperactive by grade two than kids who had a positive status with their peers (139). This factor is listed under "Societal factors" because children in general can be rejecting of any child who is different, poorly behaved, or hyperactive; hence rejection may not necessarily be specific to any one group.

Implications:

1. Children need to learn tolerance, patience and prosocial skills from adults in dealing with other children who may be different or have difficulties.

2. Children suffering from ADHD and who are aggressive are both at risk for rejection and possibly future antisocial behavior. Hence such children need early detection and intervention.

3. Even, and perhaps especially, children who are disruptive in class can be exquisitely sensitive to other's reactions to them. Their aggression may not be intentional and thus often they don't understand why they are so unpopular.

Limitations:

1. How being rejected by one's peers is actually causal or linked to further aggression is still unclear and controversial.

2. The nature of the interaction between peer rejection and other risk factors such as stress, temperament, educational achievement and discipline is still being investigated.

3. How peer rejection affects any given individual is not necessarily the same as how it statistically is noted to affect groups of children in studies.

A10. Substance Abuse

The prevalence of substance abuse in juvenile delinquents is estimated by research to be around 50% (140). A similar percentage of youth who are arrested tend to have drugs or alcohol actively circulating through their bodies at the time of arrest. The estimate of the prevalence of adolescents who are violent, have mental health problems, and abuse substances ranges between 4% and 20% (77,141,142). Many clinicians and researchers feel that the emotional difficulties in these youth precede the drug problems chronologically. However, the availability of drugs, including marijuana (the most commonly used substance) certainly enables youth who have difficulties, to attempt to mask their clinical symptoms, including those of depression, anxiety, panic, psychotic thinking or delusions, dissociation (often secondary to severe childhood abuse), attention or hyperactive problems.

Implications:

1. The over-emphasis on more overt behaviors such as drug use or violence tends to hide other treatable conditions such as the above psychiatric disorders.

2. Youth who are at risk will likely discover and use drugs as they are so readily available. The subsequent involvement in the drug subculture increases their risk of violence and criminal problems.

3. Simply assuming that violent youth are troublesome kids and sending them to short term programs or jail without addressing the reasons for their substance abuse is short sighted.

Limitations:

1. Youth who have multiple problems such as mental, educational, and addictions issues are quite complex to treat therapeutically. Hence

the tendency to use a harsh, brief, or a singular approach (e.g. boot camp) is deceptively appealing for its simplicity.

2. Substances are used by different youth for different reasons. Many of today's substance abuse treatment programs simply overlook complex underlying psychiatric issues and thus recurrence of addictions and problem behaviors is common.

3. The corrections system likely exposes the youth to even more antisocial, violent and substance-abusing behavior. Hence such a punishment often likely just exacerbates the problem.

A11. Mental illness

The contribution of mental illness towards violence in our society is certainly a popular media topic. Indeed youth who enter the juvenile justice system may be at higher risk of having a mental disorder (9), especially if one looks for Attention Deficit/Hyperactivity Disorder, Post Traumatic Stress Disorder, Depression, Substance Abuse, or a thought disorder (such as paranoid thinking in particular). Whether these contributed to the act of violence or crime is a whole other matter. There is much more research on adult offenders with mental illness. Generally in the adult group, abusing substances has been found to significantly increase risk of violence but other forms of mental illness only slightly increase risk. Having currently active symptoms has been found to be more important than simply having a diagnosis in looking at the risk for violence. It is often unclear what actually links mental illness with violence if and when a link is found in a given person.

Implications:

1. Mental illness in general confers a slightly increased risk of violence in the community. However, abusing substances is a much more potent risk factor for violence.

2. Youth and adults with any identifiable mental disorder need identification and treatment, even if their symptoms were not related to the crime with which they are charged.

3. Compared to the risk of violence due to male gender, age (adolescence or young adulthood), and economic influences, the risk of violence due to mental illness is small indeed.

Limitations:

1. Even though having an active mental illness, particularly when coupled with substance abuse increases risk of violence slightly, the vast majority (well over 90%) of people who have a mental illness are not violent.

2. Most crimes are not committed by people with a serious and persistent mental illness, such as the examples given above.

3. The sensationalization of the link between mental illness and violence only serves to pander to public fears; however, this illusion will likely continue as it provides a ready scapegoat that detracts from larger and more complex societal issues. Living in an economically impoverished, crime-ridden neighborhood is much more dangerous than living next door to someone with a mental illness.

B1. Marriage

Marriage is often listed under protective factors that decrease the suicide or violence risk in families (74). Certainly group research concludes that people who are married generally report greater happiness and longevity compared to those who are single. Marriage is also thought to provide greater resources and stability for children of the relationship. Many people believe that the increase in relationship breakdown and divorce and the attendant difficulties for children are contributing to the prevalence of childhood behavioral disorders in our society. Finally, there is very strong evidence that young, single, poor, socially isolated mothers are one of the highest, if not the highest risk group with respect to having aggressive or violent children (78). However, having repeated or continuous open conflict in a marriage can easily outweigh the benefits marriage provides.

Implications:

1. Throughout history, a stable relationship has proved advantageous in terms of provision of economic, social, and supportive resources for children.

2. Dealing with conflict in marriage in non-aggressive ways that don't involve the children is likely just or even more protective than simply being legally married.

3. Single parents, especially impoverished ones, often need extra attention, support, and resources relative to two parent families. Parenting is extremely demanding as well as rewarding, and extra help is usually beneficial for the children to reduce parental stress.

Limitations:

1. We previously noted that early marriage in a parent can be a risk factor for increasing childhood behavioral problems. Conflict-ridden or violent relationships are also detrimental for children. Thus the quality of the marriage is likely more important than the fact of having two physically present parents.

2. There are many parents who do very well as single parents due to maturity, connection with the child, emotional stability and/or access to resources.

3. Group data that stresses marriage as a protective factor doesn't usually quantify or qualify which characteristics of marriage make it protective. This understanding is necessary to guide prevention efforts and marital therapy approaches.

B2. Early childhood education

Generally, the earlier the approach, the greater the likelihood of success. Hence, it has been found that preschool programs can be effective in helping children reduce aggressive behavior, especially if language development is a strong focus of the program (143). The strongest findings have emerged for those preschool programs that also have a significant family component (home visits and/or parenting training). This is a different finding than research has shown for day care. Some researchers have found that children involved in day care for more than 20 hours per week, beginning in their first year of life, can be more aggressive, irritable, and non-compliant. However, continued aggression, non-compliance and behavior problems have not been shown in these children past early elementary school. In any event, greater government and policy support for universal early childhood education may greatly reduce the violence potential of the next generation.

Implications:

1. The combination of early childhood education and parenting classes and support can be highly protective in decreasing later aggressive difficulties in children.

2. Finding a preschool with a good reputation that nurtures children, stresses language and cognitive development, and has teacher-led, student-initiated and student-focussed activities can be challenging but worthwhile.

3. Combining preschool with learning about effective parenting will likely reinforce the child's socialization, discipline, and cognitive development.

Limitations:

1. A lot of the research in this area was done many years ago. We have a different society and demographics now. For example, having home visits would be more difficult if parents are working hard to support their families and thus not at home.

2. It is unclear whether addressing family factors and early childhood education alone, without looking at neighborhood factors (drugs, guns, gangs, poverty etc.) can effect long term change in violence potential.

3. Most studies have not randomly assigned children to day care thus leaving the possibility that the poor results for day care are biased.

B3. Mentoring

It was previously discussed that for children and youth, having a stable, trusting relationship with an adult (who is competent and a good role model) can be protective. The idea behind mentoring is providing such a person to foster a supportive relationship with a youth. The program that has been most strongly endorsed through evaluation is the Big Brother/Big Sister program. The essential ingredients thought to contribute to its success as a mentoring program include a high level of contact between the youth and adult, good screening of volunteers, orientation and training of prospective candidates, and the support of professional workers in the organization. Evaluation in eight cities revealed that youth involved with this program were less likely to initiate substance use, alcohol use, and aggressive behavior by 46%, 27%, and 31% respectively; truancy was also reduced (144). Hence societal support for such agencies is vital.

Implications:

1. Well-organized mentoring programs such as the Big Brother/Big Sister program can positively influence the rate of aggression and antisocial behavior in involved youth.

2. Youth at risk are often isolated or associate with delinquent peers. Having a competent adult, assuming one is available, can be a real adjunct to other efforts to keep the youth on track.

3. The match between youth and adult is very important. Hence screening and training of volunteers, and a good rapport is vital. Otherwise results will likely be less encouraging.

Limitations:

1. Many lesser known mentoring programs have not been scientifically evaluated. Hence it is difficult to say how effective they truly are.

2. Long-term follow-up is necessary to determine whether mentoring programs really make a difference over time. Many programs (as we saw for short-term recreation programs) may make short term gains which are lost over time. In fact, some programs have been linked to increased delinquent outcomes!

3. Mentoring programs need a fair amount of organization and structure for effectiveness. Such issues as matching the youth to adult, screening, training, supporting the adult, scheduling contact, maintaining regular contact, building trust and rapport all require intense devotion and dedication on the part of both the program and its volunteers.

B4. *Volunteering*

Society uses volunteers for many purposes. We have already alluded to the possibility of society's talented retired persons and others being involved in leisure programs for youth after school. Also, volunteers help decrease social isolation, a risk factor by itself that can contribute to parental stress and poor outcomes for children. Research has also found that specific times are particular hot spots for conflict between children and parents. Examples include mealtimes, completing tasks, chores, getting ready for school, and sibling fighting. Some research is also suggesting that community volunteers (or even videotapes about parenting for that matter) can be as effective as professionals in helping parents cope and deal with their children at these and other problematic moments (145,146). Hence a greatly underutilized societal resource would be having volunteers, particularly retired persons, teach, mentor and support parenting programs to isolated and conflictual families with disruptive children.

Implications:

1. Mental health professionals will likely never be able to reach all parents who need parenting support. Hence training volunteers in proven parenting techniques so they can reach others would accomplish violence prevention on a much broader scale.

2. Families often mistrust professionals. People often relate better to those who are not deemed "experts". Hence a volunteer may have much better rapport with a family and thus be potentially more effective.

3. As our population ages, the numbers of retired persons will increase. What better resource to help with the younger generation than experienced volunteers who are likely less threatening than agencies or professionals.

Limitations:

1. Whether many or most retired persons will actually want to be involved in such ventures is not known. Many people who have worked hard their whole lives simply want and deserve to relax in their later years.

2. Teaching parenting can be tricky as differing opinions about practices occur. A common example is corporal punishment (spanking). This was more common when retired persons were parents but less accepted now, due to evidence of worse long term effects on aggression in children.

3. Organization of such a program involving high risk families and volunteers using proven parenting and child management techniques would require clear leadership, vision, energy, and support from agencies and governments.

CONCLUSIONS

Several major points are salient with regards to violence prevention:

1. This is not a simple task. Multiple risk and protective factors occur simultaneously. To be truly successful at reducing a child or youth's risk, one needs to address as many risk factors and augment as many protective factors as possible.

2. Research, while striving to be informative, can also be unclear, controversial, difficult to implement, or of questionable standards, making conclusions difficult. However, to move forward, we do need solid evidence to address the many and complicated variables that influence aggressive youth today, and to support our interventions tomorrow.

3. To truly influence a child's life requires a look at the big picture. Examining biological, psychological, social, familial, and societal factors that operate concurrently and interactively will enrich and broaden our ability to serve that child and family.

4. We don't have all the answers. While there are some things that help, there is no panacea. This again stresses the need to look at the whole situation, no matter how complex.

5. This book was written to inform everyone, but especially those at the grass roots level who deal directly with aggressive children. If we are ever to make a dent in children's lives, those closest to them need accurate information and support to make a difference.

6. Many people look for groups or single issues to blame when there is a violent tragedy. The parents, schools, youth, drugs, guns, gangs, the media, and society are all typical targets of our outrage and tendency to point the finger. However, hopefully the discussion enclosed served to illustrate that all of these factors and more contribute in a meaningful way to human behavior, and thus rarely if ever does one dimension of a person or environment explain everything.

7. Much of violent behavior is influenced by context or situations which cannot be predicted. In retrospect we tend to look back and say that we can identify things that led to a homicide or assault. However, predicting if and when such a crime will happen is fraught with problems and inaccuracies. Hence while we may know a lot about what influences behavior, we can never possibly predict or know all combinations of individual, family, biological, environmental and situational risk factors that interact to produce antisocial behavior.

8. We need more research, understanding and application of protective factors to truly positively influence children's lives. Focussing primarily on risk alone is insufficient.

9. Violence is unfortunately a very persistent and enduring part of our heritage as human beings. Anthropologists and historians have documented violent behavior in most races, cultures, civilizations, and societies, whether human or animal. We can certainly strive to understand it more scientifically. However, we are a violent species; while we are capable of great strivings as humans, we are also capable of great destruction and suffering. This is the paradoxical nature of humanity. I wouldn't be so fatalistic to pronounce that we just have to live with it as we always have, but the unfortunate truth is

that it is one of the things that defines who we are. Nevertheless, recognizing that and working on reducing the likelihood of aggression while increasing the potential of each human being will move us forward as a society.

Lindley Bassarath, MD

REFERENCES

1. J. McCord & M. Ensminger (1995): "Pathways from aggressive childhood to criminality". This was a paper presented at the American Society of Criminology, Boston.

2. T. Moffitt (1993): "Adolescence-Limited and Life-Course Persistent Antisocial Behavior: A Developmental Taxonomy." Psychological Review 100:674-701.

3. R.D. Parke & R.G. Slaby (1983): The development of aggression. In P. Mussen (Ed.), Handbook of Child Psychology (pp. 547-642). New York: Wiley.

4. R. Sampson & J. Laub (1992): Crime and deviance in the life course. Annual Review of Sociology, 18:63-84

5. D. P. Farrington (1989): "Early predictors of adolescent aggression and adult violence". In: Violence and Victims, 4, pages 79-100.

6. K.A. Dodge & J.D. Coie (1987): Social information-processing factors in reactive and proactive aggression in children's playgroups. Journal of Personality and Social Psychology, 53, 1146-1158.

7. N.R. Crick & J.K. Grotpeter (1985): Relational aggression, gender, and social-psychological adjustment. Child Development 66, 710-722.

8. M. Lipsey & J.H. Derzon (1998): "Predictors of Serious Delinquency in Adolescence and Early Adulthood: A Synthesis of Longitudinal Research". In: Serious and Violent Juvenile Offenders:

Risk Factors and Successful Interventions, edited by R. Loeber and DP Farrington. Thousand Oaks, Calif.: Sage

9. C.A. Yeager & D.O. Lewis (Oct. 2000): " Mental Illness, Neuropsychologic Deficits, Child Abuse, and Violence". In: Child and Adolescent Psychiatric Clinics of North America, Volume 9, pages 793-813.

10. L. DeMilio (1989): Psychiatric syndromes in adolescent substance abusers. American Journal of Psychiatry 146, 1212-1214.

11. L.N. Robins & D.A. Regier (Eds.). (1991): Psychiatric disorders in America: The Epidemiologic Catchment Area study. New York: Free Press.

12. J.J. Collins & P.M. Messerschmidt (1993): Epidemiology of alcohol-related violence. In: Alcohol Health & Research World, 17, pages 93-100.

13. C.R. Cloninger, M. Bohman & S. Sigvardsson (1981): "Inheritance of alcohol abuse: Cross-fostering analysis of adopted men". In: Archives of General Psychiatry, 52, pages 916-924.

14. C. Webster-Stratton (1992): "The Incredible Years—A Trouble-Shooting Guide for Parents of Children Aged 3-8". Umbrella Press, Toronto.

15. A. Sanson, D. Smart, M. Prior, and F. Oberklaid (1993): "Precursors of Hyperactivity and Aggression". In: Journal of the American Academy of Child and Adolescent Psychiatry, Number 32, pages 1207-1216.

16. T. E. Moffitt (1990): Juvenile delinquency and attention-deficit disorder: Developmental trajectories from age 3 to 15. In: Child Development 61: pages 893-910.

17. F. Esbensen & D.W. Osgood (1997): "National Evaluation of Gang Resistance and Education Training Research in Brief". US Department of Justice, National Institute of Justice, Washington D.C.

18. E Maguin, J.D. Hawkins, R.F. Catalano, K. Hill, R. Abbott & T. Herrenkohl (1995): "Risk factors measured at three ages for violence at age 17-18". Presented at the American Society of Criminology, Boston.

19. A. Raine, C. Reynolds, P.H. Venables, S.A. Mednick & D. Farrington (1998): Fearlessness, Stimulation-Seeking, and Large Body Size at Age 3 as Early Predispositions to Childhood Aggression at Age 11 Years. Archives of General Psychiatry 55: 745-751.

20. J.H. Williams (1994): "Understanding substance use, delinquency involvement, and juvenile justice system involvement among African-American and European-American adolescents". University of Washington, Seattle.

21. Q. Zhang, R. Loeber & M. Stouthamer-Loeber (1997): "Developmental trends of delinquency attitudes and delinquency: Replication and synthesis across time and samples". In: Journal of Quantitative Criminology, 13, pages 181-216.

22. H.N. Snyder & M. Sickmund (1995): Juvenile offenders and victims: A national report. Washington, DC: Office of Juvenile Justice and Delinquency Prevention.

23. R. Loeber & D.P. Farrington (1997): "Strategies and Yields of Longitudinal Studies on Antisocial Behavior". In: D.M. Stoff, J. Breiling, J.D. Maser (editors): Handbook of Antisocial Behavior, pages 125-139. John Wiley & Sons (Publishers).

24. J.M. Wootton, P.J. Frick, K.K. Shelton, P. Silverthorn (1997): Ineffective parenting and childhood conduct problems: The moderating role of callous-unemotional traits. Journal of Consulting & Clinical Psychology. Vol 65(2), 292-300.

25. D.M. Svrakic, C. Whitehead, T.R. Przybeck & C.R. Cloninger (1993): "Differential diagnosis of personality disorders by the seven factor model of temperament and character". In: Archives of General Psychiatry, 50, pages 991-999.

26. J. Osofsky (1997): Children in a Violent Society. New York, Guilford.

27. B.J. Bushman & R.F. Baumeister (1998): "Threatened egotism, narcissism, self-esteem, and direct and displaced aggression: Does self-love or self-hate lead to violence?". In: Journal of Personality & Social Psychology, Volume 75 (1), pages 219-222.

28. R.F. Baumeister, L. Smart & J.M. Boden (1996): Relation of threatened egoism to violence and aggression: The dark side of high esteem. Psychological Review, 103, 5-33.

29. D.S. Shaw & J.I. Vondra (1995): "Attachment security and maternal predictors of early behavior problems: A longitudinal study of low-income families". In: Journal of Abnormal Child Psychology, 23, pages 335-357.

30. R. Loeber, S.M. Green, K. Keenan & B.B. Lahey (1995): "Which boys will fare worse? Early predictors of the onset of conduct disorder in a six-year longitudinal study". In: Journal of the American Academy of Child and Adolescent Psychiatry, 34, pages 499-509.

31. R. Loeber, P. Wung, K. Keenan, and others (1993): Developmental pathways in disruptive child behavior. Development and Psychopathology 5:101-133.

32. K.A. Dodge, J.E. Lochman, J.D. Harnish, J.E. Bates & G.S. Pettit (1997): "Reactive and proactive aggression in school children and psychiatrically impaired chronically assaultive youth". In: Journal of Abnormal Psychology, 106 (1), pages 37-51.

33. A. Kazdin (Oct. 2000): "Treatments for Aggressive and Antisocial Children", in Child and Psychiatric Clinics of North America, Vol 9, No 4, pages 841-858.

34. D.S. Shaw, K. Keenan, E. Owens, E.B. Winslow, N. Hood & M. Garcia (1995): "Developmental precursors of externalizing behavior among two samples of low-income families: Ages 1 to 5". Society for Research in Child Development meeting, Indianapolis, Indiana.

35. D.M. Robbins, J. C. Beck, R. Pries and others (1983): " Learning disabilities and neuropsychological impairment in adjudicated, unincarcerated male delinquents". In: Journal of the American Academy of Child and Adolescent Psychiatry, 22: pages 40-46.

36. R.F. Catalano & J.D. Hawkins (1996). "The social development model: A theory of antisocial behaviour". In: J.D. Hawkins (Editor), Delinquency and Crime: Current Theories (pp.149-197). New York: Cambridge University Press.

37. D.W. Denno (1990). Biology and Violence: From birth to adult-hood. Cambridge, United Kingdom: Cambridge University Press.

38. D.S. Elliott (1994): Serious violent offenders: onset, developmental course and termination. In: Criminology 32: pages 1-21.

39. A. Rosenbaum & S. K. Hoge (1989): "Head injury and marital aggression". In: American Journal of Psychiatry, 146, pages 1048-1051.

40. F.A. Elliott (1982): Neurological findings in adult minimal brain dysfunction and the dyscontrol syndrome. Journal of Nervous and Mental Disease, 170, 680-687.

41. D.O. Lewis, R. Lovely, C. Yeager, G. Ferguson, M. Friedman and others (1988): Neuropsychiatric, psychoeducational and family characteristics of 14 juveniles condemned to death in the United States. American Journal of Psychiatry, 145, 584-589.

42. L.H. Haller (2000): Forensic Aspects of Juvenile Violence. Child and Adolescent Psychiatric Clinics of North America, volume 9, number 4, pages 859-881.

43. R. Schachar, Ml. Rutter, & A. Smith (1981): "The characteristics of situationally and pervasively hyperactive children: Implications: for syndrome definition". In: Journal of Child Psychology and Psychiatry, 22, pages 375-392.

44. MTA Cooperative Group (1999): A 14-month randomized clinical trial of treatment strategies for Attention Deficit Hyperactivity Disorder (ADHD). Archives of General Psychiatry, 56, 1073-1086.

45. ADAM (Arrestee Drug Abuse Monitoring Program): 1998 Annual Report on Drug Use Among Adult and Juvenile Arrestees. Washington, DC, US Department of Justice, National Institute of Justice.

46. V.M.I. Linnoila & M. Virkunnen (1992): "Aggression, suicidality and serotonin". In: Journal of Clinical Psychiatry, 53, pages 46-51.

47. M. Haney, K. Noda, R. Kream, and others (1990): Regional 5-HT and dopamine activity: Sensitivity to amphetamine and aggressive behavior in mice. Aggressive Behavior 16, 259-270.

48. N.R. Carlson (1994): "Physiology of Behavior". Boston, MA, Allyn & Bacon.

49. G.L. Brown, F.K. Goodwin, J.C. Ballenger and others (1979): "Aggression in humans correlates with cerebrospinal fluid amine metabolites". In: Psychiatry Research 1, pages 131-139.

50. D. Woodman & J. Hinton (1978): Catecholamine imbalance during stress anticipation: An abnormality in maximum security hospital patients. Journal of Psychosomatic Research 22, 477-483.

51. K.A. Miczek (1987): The psychopharmacology of aggression. In: Handbook of Psychopharmacology, Vol. 19, edited by L.L. Iversen, S.D. Iversen, and S.H. Snyder. New York: Plenum Press.

52. J. Benjamin, L. Li, C Patterson, and others (1996): "Population and familial association between the D4 dopamine receptor gene and measures of novelty seeking". In: Nature Genetics 12, pages 81-84.

53. H.G. Brunner, M. Nelen, X.O. Breakfield, H.H. Ropers & B.A. Van Oost (1993): Abnormal behavior associated with a point

mutation in the structural gene for monoamine oxidase A. In: Science, 262, pages 578-580.

54. A. Raine, P. Brennan, S.A. Mednick (1994): "Birth Complications Combined with Early Maternal Rejection at Age 1 Year Predispose to Violent Crime at Age 18 Years". In: Archives of General Psychiatry, volume 51, pages 984-988.

55. E. Kandel & S.A. Mednick (1991): Perinatal complications predict violent offending. Criminology; 29, 519-529.

56. E.E. Werner (1987): "Vulnerability and resilience in children at risk for delinquency: A longitudinal study from birth to adulthood". In: J.D. Burchard & S.N. Burchard (Editors), Primary prevention of psychopathology, pages 16-43. Newbury Park, CA: Sage Publications.

57. M. McCormick (1985): The contribution of low birth weight to infant mortality and childhood morbidity. New England Journal of Medicine, 312, 82-90.

58. S.J. Schoenthaler (1983): "Diet and delinquency: A multi-state replication". In: International Journal of Biosocial Research, 5, pages 70-78.

59. M.J. Paschall (1996): Exposure to violence and the onset of violent behavior and substance use among black male youth: An assessment of independent effects and psychosocial mediators. Paper presented at the Society for Prevention Research, San Juan PR.

60. C. Bell & E. Jenkins (1991): Traumatic stress and children. Journal of Health Care Poor Underserved 2(1): 175-185.

61. L.R. Huesmann & L.S. Miller (1994): Long-term effects of repeated exposure to media violence in childhood. In: L.R. Huesmann (Ed.), Aggressive behavior: Current perspectives (pages 153-186). New York: Plenum.

62. C.H. Hansen & R.D. Hansen (1990): "Rock music videos and anti-social behavior". In: Basic and Applied Social Psychology, 11, pages 357-369.

63. V.B. Cline, R.G. Croft, & S. Courrier (1973): Desensitization of children to television violence. Journal of Personality and Social Psychology, 27, pages 360-365.

64. L.R. Huesmann & L.D. Eron (1986): Television and the aggressive child: A cross-national comparison. Hillsdale: NJ: Erlbaum.

65. S. Mitchell & P. Rosa (1979): "Boyhood behaviour problems as precursors of criminality: A fifteen-year follow-up study". In: Journal of Child Psychology & Psychiatry 22, pages 19-33.

66. M. Zoccolillo (1992): Co-occurrence of conduct disorder and its adult outcomes with depressive and anxiety disorders: A review. Journal of the American Academy of Child and Adolescent Psychiatry, 31, pages 547-556.

67. H.M. Walker & S.R. McConnell (1996): "Walker-McConnell Scale of Social Competence and School Adjustment Manuals and Forms. San Diego, California, Singular Publishing Group.

68. F. Esbensen & D.W. Osgood (1997): "National Evaluation of Gang Resistance and Education Training Research in Brief". US Department of Justice, National Institute of Justice, Washington D.C.

69. C.R. Cloninger, T.R. Przybeck, D.M. Svrakic & R.D. Wetzel (1994): "The Temperament and Character Inventory (TCI): A guide to its development and use". St. Louis: Washington University Center for Psychobiology of Personality.

70. C. Mallar, S. Kerachsky, C. Thornton & D. Long (1982): Evaluation of the Economic Impact of the Job Corps Program, Third Follow-Up Report. Princeton, NJ.

71. G. Cave, H. Bos, F. Doolittle & C. Toussaint (1990): JOBSTART: Final Report on a Program for School Dropouts. New York: Manpower.

72. J.C. Howell, S. Bilchik, editors (1995): Guide for Implementing the Comprehensive Strategy for Serious Violent and Chronic Juvenile Offenders. Office of Juvenile Justice and Delinquency Prevention, Washington, D.C. NCJ-153681.

73. C.R. Cloninger, C. Bayon & T.R. Przybeck (1997): Epidemiology and Axis I Comorbidity of Antisocial personality. In: D.M. Stoff, J. Breiling, & J. Maser (editors), Handbook of Antisocial Behavior, chapter 2, page17, John Wiley & Sons.

74. R. Plutchik & H.M. van Praag (1990): "Psychsocial correlates of suicide and violence risk". In: H.M. van Praag, R. Plutchik, & A. Apter (Editors), Violence and suicidality: Perspectives in clinical and psychobiological research, pages 37-65. New York: Brunner/Mazel.

75. Institute of Medicine (1994).

76. A Cherlin (1993): "Marriage, Divorce and Remarriage". Cambridge, MA, Harvard University Press.

77. J. Dryfoos (1990): "Adolescents at risk". New York, Oxford University Press.

78. D.S. Nagin & R.E. Tremblay (2001): Parental and early childhood predictors of persistent physical aggression in boys from kindergarten to high school. Archives of General Psychiatry, Volume 58(4), pages 389-394.

79. D.A. Andrews, A.W. Leschied, and R.D. Hope (1992): " Review of the Profile, Classification and Treatment Literature of Young Offenders: A Social Psychological Approach". Ottawa, Canada (Carleton University) & London, Ontario, Canada (Family Court Clinic).

80. R. Brown, C.D. Coles, I.E. Smith, K.A. Platzman, J. Silverstein, S. Erickson, & A. Falek (1991): "Effects of prenatal alcohol exposure at school age: II. Attention and behavior". In: Neurotoxicology and Teratology, 13, pages 369-376.

81. NIDA (National Institute on Drug Abuse) Notes (January—February 1995). National Institute on Drug Abuse, National Institutes of Health, Bethesda MD.

82. T.E. Moffitt (1993): "Adolescence-Limited and Life-Course-Persistent Antisocial Behavior: A Developmental Taxonomy". In: Psychological Review 100, pages 674-701.

83. R.O. Pihl & F. Ervin (1990): Lead and cadmium levels in violent criminals. Psychological Reports, 66, 839-844.

84. U.S. Public Health Service Expert Panel on the Content of Prenatal Care (1989).

85. J.H. Williams (1994): "Understanding substance use, delinquency involvement, and juvenile justice system involvement among African-American and European-American adolescents". University of Washington, Seattle.

86. G.R. Patterson & M. Stouthamer-Loeber M (1984): The correlation of family management practices and delinquency. Child Development 55: 1299-1307.

87. K.J. Weintraub & M. Gold (1991): Monitoring and delinquency. Criminal Behavior and Mental Health 1: pages 268-281.

88. G.R. Patterson (1982): "Coercive Family Process". Eugene, Oregon: Castalia.

89. J. McCord (1979): Somechild-rearing antecedents of criminal behavior in adult men. Journal of Personality and Social Psychology, 37, 1477-1486.

90. L.E. Wells & J.H. Rankin (1988). Direct parental controls and delinquency. Criminology, 26, 263-285.

91. D.L Olds, J. Eckenrode, C.R. Henderson, H. Kitzman, J. Powers, R. Cole and others (1997): "Long-Term Effects of Home Visitation on Maternal Life Course and Child Abuse and Neglect: Fifteen-Year Follow-up of a Randomized Trial". In: Journal of the American Medical Association 278, pages 637-643.

92. L.D. Eron (1987): "The development of aggressive behavior from the perspective of a developing behaviorism". In: American Psychologist, 42, pages 435

93. C. Webster-Stratton (1992): "The Incredible Years—A Trouble-Shooting Guide for Parents of Children Aged 3-8". Umbrella Press, Toronto.

94. D.L. Olds & H. Kitzman (1993): "Review of Research on Home Visiting for Pregnant Women and Parents of Young Children". In: Future of Children 3, 53-92.

95. R.E. Tremblay, F. Vitaro, and others (1992): " Parent and Child Training to Prevent Early Onset of Delinquency: The Montreal Longitudinal—Experimental Study". In: Preventing Antisocial Behavior: Interventions from Birth through Adolescence, edited by J. McCord and R.E. Tremblay. New York; Guilford.

96. R.E. Slavin, N.A. Madden, and others (1995): "Success for All: A Summary of Research". American Educational Research Association meeting, San Francisco.

97. S.S. Brown, L. Eisenberg (Editors) (1995): The Best Intentions: Unintended Pregnancy and the Well-Being of Children and Families. National Academic Press, Washington D.C.

98. Kellermann, D.S. Fuqua-Whitley, F.P. Rivara, and J. Mercy (1998): "Preventing Youth Violence: What Works?" In: Annual Review of Public Health, 19: pages 271-292.

99. E. Maguin, J.D. Hawkins, R.F. Catalano and others (1995): "Risk factors measured at three ages of violence at age 17-18".American Society of Criminology, Boston.

100. N. Garmezy (1985): "Stress-Resistant Children: The Search for Protective Factors". In: Recent Research in Developmental

Psychopathology, edited by J.E. Stevenson, Journal of Child Psychology and Psychiatry (supplement), 4: pages 213-233.

101. D.S. Elliott (1994): Serious violent offenders: onset, developmental course and termination. In: Criminology 32: pages 1-21.

102. E.L. Lipman, D.R. Offord, & M.D. Dooley (1996): "What Do We Know About Children from Single-Mother families?". In: Growing Up in Canada National Longitudinal Survey of Children and Youth, pages 83-91.

103. R. Gartner & F.C. Pampel (1995): "Age structure, socio-political institutions, and national homicide rates". In: European Sociological Review 11: pages 243-260.

104. M.R. Dadds & M.B. Powell (1991): "The relationship of inter-parental conflict and global marital adjustment to aggression and immaturity in aggressive and nonclinic children". In: "Journal of Abnormal Child Psychology, 19, pages 553-567.

105. C.S. Widom (1989): "The cycle of violence". In: Science, 244, pages 160-166.

106. F. Rothbaum & J. Weisz (1994): "Parental caregiving and child externalizing behavior in nonclinical samples: A meta-analysis. In: Psychological Bulletin, 116, pages 55-74.

107. Ageton SS. Sexual assault among adolescents (1983); Lexington, MA: Lexington Books.

108. Baker RLA & Mednick BR. Influences on human development: A longitudinal perspective (1984); Boston: Kluwer-Nijhoff.

109.J. McCord (1991): " Family relationships, juvenile delinquency, and adult criminality". In: Criminology 29 pages 297-417.

110.B. Henry, C. Avshalom and others (1996): "Temperamental and familial predictors of violent and nonviolent criminal convictions: Age 3 to age 18". In: Developmental Psychology, 32, pages 614-623.

111.J.H. Williams (1994): "Understanding substance use, delinquency involvement, and juvenile justice system involvement among African-American and European-American adolescents". University of Washington, Seattle.

112.R.G. Wahler & J.E. Dumas (1989): "Attentional problems in dysfunctional mother-child interactions: An interbehavioral model. Psychological Bulletin, 105, pages 116-130.

113.C.R. Cloninger, M. Bohman & S. Sigvardsson (1981): "Inheritance of alcohol abuse: Cross-fostering analysis of adopted men". In: Archives of General Psychiatry, 52, pages 916-924.

114.J. Volavkia & L. Citrome (1998): "Aggression, Alcohol, and Other Substances of Abuse". In: Neurobiology and Clinical Views on Aggression and Impulsivity, edited by M. Maes and E. Coccaro, pages 29-41, Wiley.

115.D. LeBoef & P. Brennan (1996): "Curfew: an answer to juvenile delinquency and victimization?" In: OJJDP (Office of Juvenile Justice and Delinquency Prevention) Juvenile Justice Bulletin, pages 1-11, NCJ 159533.

116. J.D. Hawkins, R.F. Catalano, and Associates (1992): "Communities That Care: Action for Drug Abuse Prevention". San Francisco: Jossey-Bass.

117. J. Gabarino & D. Sherman (1980): "High risk neighborhoods and high-risk families: the human ecology of child maltreatment". In: Child Development 5:188-198.

118. M.B. Shure & G. Spivack (1980): "Interpersonal Problem Solving as Mediator of Behavioral Adjustment in Preschool and Kindergarten Children". In: Journal of Applied Developmental Psychology 1: 29-44.

119. M.B. Shure & G. Spivack (1980): "Interpersonal Cognitive Problem Solving". In: Fourteen Ounces of Prevention: A Casebook for Practitioners, edited by R.H. Price and others. Washington DC: American Psychological Association.

120. DD Brewer, JD Hawkins, and others (1995): "Preventing Serious, Violent, And Chronic Offending: A Review of Evaluations of Selected Strategies in Childhood, Adolescence, and the Community". In Sourcebook on Serious, Violent, and Chronic Juvenile Offenders, edited by JC Howell, B. Krisberg, and others. Thousand Oaks, Calif.:Sage.

121. A. P. Goldstein: "Teaching prosocial skills to antisocial youth" (1986) . In: "Special Education and the Criminal Justice System", edited by CM Nelson, RB Rutherford, BT Wolford. Columbus, OH, Charles E. Merrill.

122. R. L. Wideman (1979): "Implementing Values Education in a School System" In: Education Canada 19, pages 16-22.

123.P. Tolan & M. Mitchell (1989): "Families and the therapy of antisocial and delinquent behavior". In: Journal of Psychotherapy and Family 6: pages 29-48.

124.L.W. Shannon (1988): "Changing Patterns of Delinquency and Crime: A Longitudinal Study in Racine". New York: Human Sciences Press.

125.D.O. Carrigan (1998): Juvenile Delinquency in Canada: A History, pages 309-311. Irwin Publishing.

126.J. Richters & P. Martinez (1993): The NIMH community violence project: children as victims and witnesses to violence. Psychiatry 56:7-21.

127.M.B. Jones & D.R. Offord (1989): "Reduction of Antisocial Behavior in Poor Children by Nonschool Skill-Development". In: Journal of Child Psychology and Psychiatry and Allied Disciplines 30: pp. 737-750.

128.D.J. Flannery & C.R. Huff, editors (1999): Youth Violence: Prevention, Intervention, and Social Policy, pages 57-59. American Psychiatric Press.

129.L.J. Krivo & R.D. Peterson (1996): "Extremely Disadvantaged Neighborhoods and Urban Crime". In: Social Forces 75: pages 619-650.

130.RK Merton (1963): Social Structure and Anomie. In: Social Theory and Social Structure, pages 131-1000. New York Free Press.

131.R.J. Sampson & J.H. Laub (1994): "Urban Poverty and the Family Context of Delinquency". In: Child Development 65: pages 538-545.

132. W.J. Wilson (1991) :"Studying inner-city social dislocation". In: American Sociological Review 56: pages 1-14.

133. Center for Disease Control and Prevention (1994): Weapon carrying among high-school students, United States, 1990. Morbidity and Mortality Weekly Report, 40(40), pages 681-684.

134. J.H. Sloan, A.L. Kellerman, D.T. Reay (1988): Handgun regulations, crime, assaults, and homicides: a tale of two cities. New England Journal of Medicine 319: pages 1256-1262.

135. G. Kleck (1991): "Point Blank: Guns and Violence in America". Hawthorne, New York, Aldine de Gruyter.

136. M.W. Klein, C.L. Maxson & J. Miller (Editors) (1995): "The modern gang reader". Los Angeles: Roxbury.

137. M. Warr: "Organization and Instigation in Delinquent Groups" (1996). In: Criminology 34: pages 11-37.

138. D. Olweus: "Bully/Victim Problems among Schoolchildren: Basic Facts and Effects of a School-Based Intervention Programme" (1991). In: The Development and Treatment of Childhood Aggression, edited by D.J. Pepler and K.H. Rubin. Hillsdale, N.J.: Erlbaum.

139. F. Vitaro, R. Tremblay, C. Gagnon, & M. Boivin (1992): "Peer rejection from kindergarten to grade 2: Outcomes, correlates, and prediction". In: Merrill-Palmer Quarterly, 38, pages 382-400.

140. D. Dawson & J. Reiter (1998): Juvenile violence overview. American Academy of Psychiatry and Law Newsletter 23: 10-11.

141.P. Ellickson, H. Saner & K. McGuigan (1997): Profiles of violent youth: Substance use and other concurrent problems. American Journal of Public Health 87: 985-991.

142.D.S. Elliot, D. Huzinga, S. Menard: Multiple Problem Youth (1989): Delinquency, Substance Use and Mental Health Problems. New York, Springer-Verlag.

143.H. Yoshikawa (1995): "Long-term Effects of Early Childhood Programs on Social Outcomes and Delinquency". In: Future of Children 5: pages 51-75.

144.J.B. Grossman & E.M. Garry (April 1997): "Mentoring—A Proven Delinquency Prevention Strategy". In: Juvenile Justice Bulletin, US Dept. of Justice.

145.RE Jester & BJ Guinagh (1983): "The Gordon parent education infant and toddler program, in As the Twig Is Bent, the Lasting Effects of Preschool Programs. Edited by the Consortium for Longitudinal Studies. Hillsdale, NJ, Lawrence Erlbaum, Pages 103-132.

146.C. Webster-Stratton (1994): "Advancing videotape parent training: A comparative study". In: Journal of Consulting and Clinical Psychology, 62, pages 583-593.

INDEX

ABOUT THE AUTHOR

Dr. Lindley Bassarath is a practicing child, adolescent, and adult psychiatrist. He achieved both his medical degree and psychiatry specialty training at the University of Toronto. He has worked in the area of human conflict and aggression for many years. His interests have included custody and access disputes, mental health aspects of child welfare, and the risks and needs of juvenile delinquents. Currently he acts as a psychiatric consultant for juvenile courts. He has a private practice which includes HIV psychiatry and general psychotherapy. He also provides psychiatric outreach via telepsychiatry consultation (via broadband technology) services to under-serviced communities. He is heavily involved in teaching at the undergraduate and postgraduate university levels. Dr. Bassarath lives in Toronto, Ontario, Canada with his wife and son.